Water in a Small Garden

THE ROYAL HORTICULTURAL SOCIETY

Water in a Small Garden

John Carter

DK

LONDON, NEW YORK, MUNICH, MELBOURNE, DELHI

SENIOR EDITOR Zia Allaway
SENIOR DESIGNERS Rachael Smith,
Vanessa Hamilton
MANAGING EDITOR Anna Kruger
MANAGING ART EDITOR Alison Donovan
DTP DESIGNER Louise Waller
PICTURE RESEARCH Lucy Claxton,
Richard Dabb, Mel Watson
PRODUCTION CONTROLLER Rebecca Short

PRODUCED FOR DORLING KINDERSLEY
Airedale Publishing Limited
CREATIVE DIRECTOR Ruth Prentice
PRODUCTION MANAGER Amanda Jensen

PHOTOGRAPHY Mark Winwood

First published in Great Britain in 2007 by
Dorling Kindersley Ltd
Penguin Books Ltd
80 Strand
London WC2R 0RL

2 4 6 8 10 9 7 5 3

ISBN 9781405315944

Reproduced by Colourscan, Singapore
Printed and bound in Singapore by Star Standard

Discover more at
www.dk.com

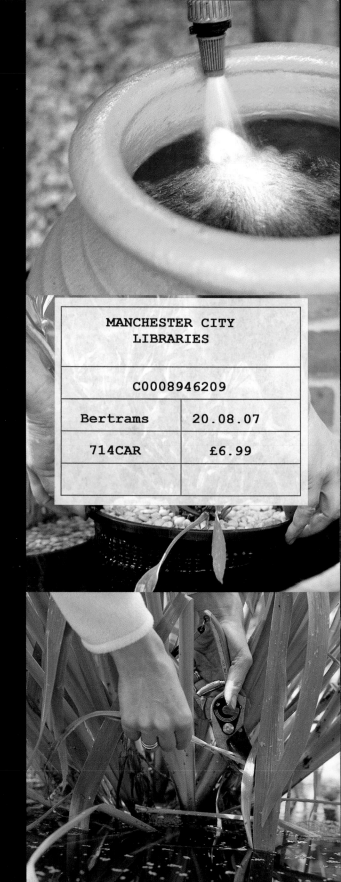

Contents

Why feature water?

Water has a magical allure, bringing light, sound and movement into a small garden. The reflections in a still pool mirror colours and shapes, while cascades and fountains dance with sparkling sunlight. Water also attracts a wealth of wildlife, providing frogs, toads and newts with a place to live, and birds with a bath. Fish offer additional colour and interest, while dragonflies and other insects will perform aerial displays above the surface. For more on these and other inspiration ideas, look through this chapter and find out how to transform your plot into a water wonderland.

Natural water features

Water in the garden creates mirrors, enhances the environment, and provides movement and sound. To look natural, a water feature must appear to be in complete harmony with its surroundings. The trick is to imitate nature as closely as possible.

Pictures clockwise from top left

Natural cascade Water flowing over these rocky outcrops creates movement and sound. The natural look comes from laying the stones horizontally, which is how they would invariably appear. This is an example of where it is easy to go wrong – if any of the stones had been placed vertically, the effect would have been destroyed.

Pebble beach A sloping, beach-like pond edge is not only attractive, but it also allows wildlife to reach the water safely. A pebble beach does need to be planned in advance, though, rather than added after the pond is installed. To meld a scattering of stones naturally into the design, place them close together at the water's edge and intersperse them with small plants further back. Behind these, a metre or so from the pond's edge, space the stones further apart or mix them in with larger cobbles.

Pond planting Aquatics, marginals, and bog plants will all thrive within a pond's close environs, but if the soil further away is dry, you will need to choose plants that look as though they belong in damp situations, but tolerate more arid conditions. Such plants include the male fern (*Dryopteris filix-mas*) and hostas, some ornamental grasses, bergenia, and lily-of-the-valley (*Convallaria majalis*), all of which have a rushy, luxurious or fern-like appearance.

Natural water features *continued*

Pictures clockwise from top left

Slate waterfall When using materials such as slate, keep the slabs parallel with the strata, and ensure the grooves in the rock follow the direction of the water flow. The rock will then look as though it has weathered naturally.

Colourful carpet Natural streams often have densely planted edges. Here, a bog garden has been planted either side of the water. Simulate this in your garden, where your "stream" will actually be a narrow, elongated pond.

Stepping stones A useful adjunct to a pond, stepping stones enhance its appearance, allow you to get close to plants, and provide perching places for wildlife. Make sure, however, that their surfaces do not become slippery. Wooden steps can be covered with wire netting.

Wildlife havens All ponds are havens for wildlife, such as frogs, toads, newts, and birds, but the more informal they are, the better. Plentiful planting, easy accessibility for wildlife, and time to allow the environment to develop are all key to creating the ideal retreat. Plants with plenty of flowers will attract insects and butterflies, and so provide a useful source of food for amphibians, but it is a fallacy that only native plant species should be used, since many of these can be very invasive, especially in small ponds.

Formal water features

For a formal look, combine the delights of water with architectural structures, either modern or traditional, depending on the style of the garden. Associated planting, exuberant or sparse, should enhance but not hide the water feature.

Pictures clockwise from left

Minimalist chic Simple and serene, this minimalist pool features only a couple of half-hardy plants, chosen for their structural qualities, to give interest to the water. For such an arrangement to succeed, careful attention will need to be paid to the conditioning of the water and the amount of light available to plants. If you need chemicals to maintain water clarity, avoid those that are copper-based.

Steady flow Lush and generous planting often combines well with moving water features. Here, a dense carpet of foliage plants, including hostas and ivies (*Hedera*), sit above a cascade of water that emerges from under the brick coping. A cascade also creates a humid atmosphere, ideal for growing ferns. This type of feature is especially suitable for small or medium-sized town gardens.

Lily pond This classic design features a rectangular pond, its shape emphasized by the paved edging and surrounding lawn. A more minimalist look could be achieved by using water hawthorn (*Aponogeton distachyos*) with the water lilies.

Raised pool In this pool, the water and the plants are brought closer to eye level. Here, the bed at the back of the L-shaped pond has been raised as well. This arrangement is particularly suited to a small garden, where a clean pond outline will help create an impression of more space.

Formal water features *continued*

Pictures clockwise from top left

Courtyard classicism A classical statue adorns a small, semi-circular water feature that is framed by simple but interesting planting in this neat courtyard. The aubergine- coloured pool, white walls, and arum lilies (*Zantedeschia aethiopica*) make a striking contrast. Such a scheme could be modified to suit similar patio or courtyard gardens.

Cool and contemporary Here, a raised pool with a white surround is used to display water as an ornament in its own right. The clean lines are emphasized by a range of subtropical plants with lush green and purple-tinged foliage that is highlighted by the white surroundings.

Patio pool This large, rectangular pool dominates the patio, providing a secluded, calm area in which to relax. Although plants frame the pool, there are few growing in it, so a cleaning system would be necessary to keep the water clear.

Sunken treasure A peaceful spot at the end of a low-lying part of the garden is a natural place for a pond. A few striking structural plants soften the brickwork and hang over the edge of the pool, creating a little sunken hideaway. Attention needs to be given to the availability of light here – plants that like shade will do best. In addition, the issue of drainage for a pond in such a position needs to be carefully considered at the planning stages to ensure that it does not fill up with rainwater and flood the patio.

Contemporary features

Modern materials and technology allow you to vent your imagination to the full. The only constraints are maintaining the right conditions for plants to grow well and the basic practicalities of upkeep.

Pictures clockwise from top left

Letterbox feature Not only is this modern take on a fountain amusing to look at, it is also pleasing to listen to, as the water streams through the letterbox opening. If you decide to create this feature for yourself, remember to use well-treated wood for the back. The metal grille prevents leaves from falling into the pool.

Bubble fountain A submerged fountain that bubbles gently on the surface makes an entertaining feature in a small, awkward space. Here, the grey pebble surround and use of a water mister make the installation look like a natural geyser and provide movement and interest in all weathers. As with any feature involving running water, you will need to keep an eye out for the effects of evaporation.

Wall of water Modern materials, such as curved stainless steel, can be used to create a dramatic wall of water that brings both movement and sound to your garden. Such a feature is particularly suitable for a small space, where there is not enough room for more conventional structures. Bear in mind that the steel will need regular cleaning and the water sterilized for the feature to retain its good looks.

Curved canal This semi-circular canal with its piped water and fountains adds a cool, refreshing note to the surrounding dry, Mediterranean-style garden.

Mirrored water To create this exciting design with its square gravity-fed voids, you will need to call in professional help. However, you could emulate the smooth reflective surfaces by installing a still pool, where the lush planting appears to be emerging from a mirrored surface. Such an effect can be greatly enhanced by incorporating real mirrors into the design by placing them vertically against a wall behind the pool, doubling the reflections.

Contemporary features *continued*

Pictures clockwise from left

Reflective surfaces This minimalist water feature adds movement and reflections to a modern garden. The water glides over the top creating a mirror-like surface – a smaller version would work well on a patio.

Baubles and domes This brightly coloured extravaganza would make a lively talking point in a part of the garden where entertaining takes place. The steel fountain domes and the glass baubles will need frequent cleaning to maintain the effect.

Five birds in a row Water gardens, like any other form of garden, can be enlivened with the use of figures, which keep their interest even when the plants have died down in the winter.

Minimalist pool A contemporary pool fills this patio garden with reflected light, while the fountain provides movement. The feature's clean lines and simple shape are integral to the garden's minimalist design.

Tapping into modernism An arched steel pipe adds the pleasing sound of flowing water as well as useful oxygen to an up-to-date pond setting.

Steel steps Combining two distinct materials, such as wood and metal, creates a striking modern design. The broad steps mean that evaporation will be fairly high.

Wall features and patio pools

Tiny water features can create a big impact in small spaces. These imaginative ideas prove the point, but bear in mind that to work properly, they all need maintenance and the light levels must be adequate for the plants you choose.

Pictures clockwise from left

Zen garden Japanese design is more complicated than it looks. If you don't have the right conditions for growing certain plants, like the high humidity required by moss, try using similar-looking plants, such as mossy saxifrages or small corydalis, which are happier in drier conditions. The water chain in the foreground will itself create some humidity.

Rustic container An old wooden barrel can create the ideal conditions for growing small water lilies (*Nymphaea*), but they will need full sun and warmth to really thrive. Be prepared to prune the water lilies in the spring, after their second year.

Lion's head In a confined space, this classical lion's head makes an eye-catching feature. It is important to keep the associated planting simple. Here, ivy (*Hedera*) makes a good covering for the wall, but beware the larger-growing varieties. The arum lily (*Zantedeschia*) in the foreground has bold, simple leaves and scented flowers. It will need to be protected in winter with a deep mulch.

Contemporary spouts Modern architecture demands innovative and up-to-date features. The pipes in clear plastic spouts are powered by a medium-sized pump. They create an excellent waterfall effect, producing plenty of movement as well as a pleasing sound. Check and top up water levels in the reservoir regularly because this installation will be subject to high evaporation (an empty reservoir will damage the pump).

Stone globes If you have a small patio, consider a simple, striking water feature. These stone globes are placed over a reservoir and the surrounding planting is small and sparse, so it doesn't compete with the sculptural feature. A small pump produces just enough water flow to be noticeable and brings the design alive.

Wall features and patio pools *continued*

Pictures clockwise from top left

Recycled vessels This old-fashioned sink fits perfectly into the corner of the garden. For the best results, it needs to be filled with plants that all require the same depth of water; alternatively, you could raise or lower the pots of plants with different needs on stones or bricks.

Timber effects Old planks of wood have been used to make this simple wall feature and to clad the pool. For a more contemporary feel, you could try using metal sheeting instead of wood.

Copper bowls A small copper feature fits into a compact space, although room is needed to hide the pump and water reservoir. Keep an eye on diminishing water levels caused by evaporation so that the pump doesn't run dry.

Self-contained fountains There are many designs to suit all types of garden. Although easy to install, the electricity supply must be connected by a qualified electrician. Maintenance is minimal: remove any leaves from the water, and disconnect the pump and bring it indoors over winter.

Fountains and rills

Rills and fountains demonstrate the versatility of water in a range of situations. They all exploit water's unique qualities in some way to create different moods or effects: movement or tranquillity, sound or silence, excitement or serenity. With ingenuity, water features such as these can be installed relatively cheaply.

Pictures clockwise from top left

Curtain call All the qualities of water are celebrated in this appealing feature. The water makes its own music as it streams down, splashing into the pool, and catches the light to create a curtain of colour. Being hidden behind the waterfall evokes a feeling of intimacy and seclusion but also one of excitement as you peer through the curtain to the garden beyond.

Classic cherub The antique appearance of this stone cherub offers a sense of maturity to the newest garden. When placed on the edge of a small pool, it has the added advantage of aerating the water.

Islamic rill Inspired by natural rivers and lakes, this simply designed Islamic rill is seen here in formal surroundings. Similar shallow pools and rills can be used in endless variations to suit small town gardens and patios.

Rustic effect The idea of a stream of water contained within a simple metal trough-like rill is useful in a small garden where a rustic effect is desired.

Snaking stream This modern design incorporates bold and restful curves that are emphasized by the gleaming tranquil water. A pump gently pushes the water through the garden, but to maintain water quality in such a design, you may have to use chemicals or incorporate an ultraviolet filter into the pumping system.

Copper fountain Using metal for the construction of contemporary water features produces many striking effects. The metal you use, though, must be specially treated to prevent oxidization, otherwise regular cleaning and polishing will be necessary. Copper is, perhaps, an exception, and turns an attractive blue-green when in contact with the air.

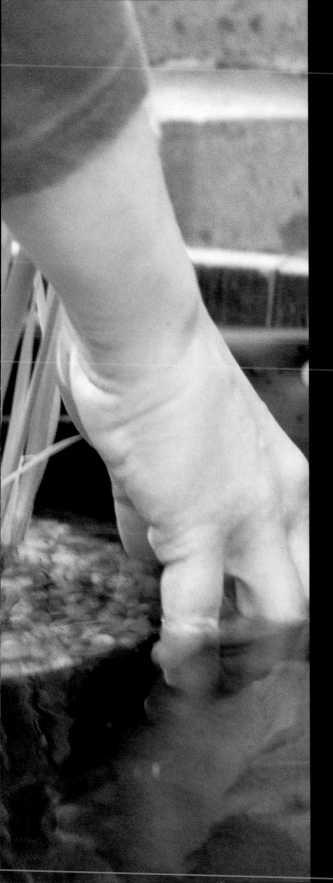

Getting started

Before building a water feature, consider the proposed size and cost to make sure that it is right for your garden and your budget. Even small gardens can accommodate large features, such as a wildlife pond or cascade, although a pool of more limited proportions would suit a tiny plot or part of a larger scheme. This chapter outlines the benefits of each type of water feature, and shows a range of liners and edging options to choose from. If you would like a moving water feature, there are sections on pumps, filters and waterfalls, and for a night-time display, look at the pages on lighting. The best soils and containers for aquatic plants are described at the end of the chapter.

Choosing a large water feature

Pools and ponds make very attractive features in small gardens, turning even tiny plots into watery oases. The options given here show a range of styles.

Informal pond

This kind of pool merges naturally into your garden, making a harmonious contribution to a wildlife, meadow-style, or other informal garden design.

Best for The most suitable positions for this kind of water feature emphasize the feeling of informality. The pond can be installed in front of a rockery, or within a flower bed or shrubbery, or placed by a path through a wild garden. Build a pond where reflections can create some impact.

Construction Simplicity is the keynote. Rigid liners can be used, but the edges must be disguised to maintain the natural look. Avoid complicated shapes if you are using a flexible butyl liner, because not only are inlets and islands difficult to construct, they will also destroy the effect. Make sure that rain can't wash soil into the pond.

Planting Don't be over enthusiastic in your plant choices. Find out what plants will suit your pond and avoid those that are too robust or invasive. Ensure the water you have spent time and money putting into place can be seen easily.

Aftercare If properly installed, an informal pond needs little aftercare. Keep an eye out for annual and perennial weeds, cut out dead foliage, and remove seedheads. Clear out the sludge in the bottom every four years or so.

Raised formal pool

A raised pool with decorative surroundings will form a beautiful feature in its own right. The impact of the formal pond will depend on its architectural shape and, in general, this should not be obscured. If you have a circle, ensure the edges are clearly visible; if you have a rectangle, likewise. Additions, such as fountains, statuary, and waterfalls, should also suit the formal geometry of the pool and maintain its character.

Best for This kind of pond suits the middle of a lawn, courtyard or patio, or by a wall – anywhere, in fact, where its definite shape can be suitably framed by other straight or curved lines, which may take the form of hedging, brick, or stonework.

Construction A formal pool can be made from scratch by building a shape to your own design, from brick or stone, and then lining it with butyl, or by fitting a rigid fibreglass pond of the right shape. Make sure that your structure has strong, firm foundations and that you plan power supplies in advance if you need them.

Planting In general, very simple planting is best for a formal pond. Few plants should be used and these need to be chosen to appeal for as long a season as possible. Avoid tall plants in circular formal ponds; water lilies are usually more suitable here.

Aftercare Remove any dead foliage and, after four years or so, be prepared to take out, prune, then replant the best pieces of your water lilies in fresh soil. Do this in early spring. Control annual and perennial weeds, otherwise seeds will blow about and spread.

Cascade

Water spilling down an artificial cascade provides one of the most attractive water features for a small garden. It produces natural sound and movement and complements most surroundings. Cascades also give the impression of taking up more space than they actually occupy, and make small gardens appear bigger. Cascades come in a variety of styles: the one illustrated below is informal and naturalistic, but formal constructions are just as much fun.

Best for Although a waterfall looks good in a large landscaped garden, the idea can be modified in style and scale to suit very small places as well. A cascade adds great interest to courtyards and patios, for instance.

Construction Cascades are most effective if the fall is broken and irregular, so you will need to arrange rocks or other structural elements to achieve this. It is important that you install the right pump; to do this, you will need to know the height of the header tank at the top of the cascade above the pool (see p.41).

Planting While damp-loving plants can often be inserted into crevices, it is usually best to rely on plants placed in the soil outside the edges of your cascade. Choose ferns and perhaps hostas for shady cascades, and more sun-loving subjects if your waterfall is in the open.

Aftercare A cascade will lose a lot of water through evaporation and you need to keep an eye on the water level, and top it up as necessary. From time to time, clean out fallen leaves, which can block the channel. Switch off and remove the pump for the winter.

Contemporary sunken pool

A sunken pool allows you to view water from above, and by combining a simple scheme with the use of modern materials, you can exploit the smallest spaces in a delightful way. Looking at the water and plants from above gives you a whole new perspective. The water will attract wildlife, too, so make sure that frogs and insects can get out as well as in by providing ledges around the edge. You can also grow interesting plants in this setting.

Best for Sunken pools make good points of interest anywhere, but they are most suited to contemporary or formal spaces. In particular, they make an excellent adjunct to seating areas in the garden and add interest to patios, barbecue areas, as well as modern paved gardens.

Construction Quite deep excavation is required, so you will first have to check the level of the water table (see p.33). If it is high, and will present difficulties, then all you have to do is build the pond just below ground level and then raise its surroundings. Make sure that edging, brick, and tilework are built securely.

Planting The structure of this kind of feature often means that it will lie in quite deep shade, which limits your choice of aquatic plants for the water. Instead, use the surroundings for planting, and mechanical features, such as fountains and lighting, for the pond. An area of quiet, dark water is attractive in its own right, however.

Aftercare The main job is to remove fallen leaves and twigs once a month throughout the year. If there are baskets of water plants that are not thriving, move them to a sunnier position in the pond, if possible.

Choosing a small water feature

Small water features prove that you don't need a pond to grow aquatic plants – you can grow them in the tiniest space in anything that holds water.

Wall fountains

Enjoy the sound and sight of water by installing a simple device that makes it appear to spout out of a wall. Designs vary from the classical look to modern ideas.

Best for Wall fountains can be used in alleyways, at the edge of seating areas or by garden walls and beside back doors. Provided there is easy access to electricity, they make wonderfully interesting features almost anywhere.

Construction While all-in kits are available, you can also assemble your own components. The reservoir forming the base can be a stone or terracotta bowl, an old sink, or any container deep enough to take a small pump. Hoses and copper tubing are used for the connections. The spout itself is best mounted just below eye level.

Planting In most situations, planting in the bowl or reservoir should be kept to a minimum, just enough to hide the piping. Remember to take into account how much light is available when choosing plants. Climbers like clematis, jasmine, or roses, however, can be grown around the feature to good effect.

Aftercare Keep the reservoir clear of leaves and, in warm weather, be prepared to top up water levels regularly. Disconnect and remove the pump before winter sets in.

Barrel pools

These are really miniature ponds, allowing you to grow water plants where you don't have space for a full-size pool, or want to grow plants separately. A barrel pool can also be used in conjunction with a wall fountain, where it would act as the reservoir. Barrel pools are large enough to attract wildlife, including a variety of insects. They provide birds with a bath and newts with a home, so make provisions for these creatures to get in and out.

Best for Barrels can be used either to make a small water feature on their own or to form part of a scheme with other flowerpots and bowls. In addition, they can contribute to the look of an ordinary flower bed. They also look good on patios or even beside larger ponds.

Construction You need to make sure that your barrel is waterproof. This can be done by either lining it with inexpensive black PVC plastic or painting it with a sealant. Both methods will prevent any poisonous chemicals in the wood polluting the water.

Planting Use either a number of small plants or just one larger-growing specimen. Raise baskets on bricks to obtain the optimum planting depths. It is also useful to put the plants into separate baskets to prevent them becoming entangled with one another.

Aftercare Since the barrel contains a comparatively small amount of water, it is more likely to turn green. To help prevent this from happening, choose plants with wide or floating leaves that shade the water, or, if it becomes a problem, siphon out the water and replace it. Prune out dead and over-vigorous growth.

Pebble pools

In the natural world, one of the most attractive things about water is how it flows and glistens when running over pebbles and tumbled stones. You can imitate this in a small space with a pebble pool, but bear in mind that the effect is best when rounded, water-worn pebbles are used. These are readily available from garden centres in a variety of sizes and colours.

Best for You can install a pebble pool in those awkward dark corners by walls or in difficult areas on patios and in backyards, as well as in full sun beside existing ponds and water features. The only limitation will be access to the electricity supply (for this you will need to enlist professional advice and help).

Construction A pebble pool is basically a pool filled with stones, and need only be deep enough to provide a reasonable reservoir for circulating water, with a small, submersible pump feeding a spout to direct the water over the stones. Alternatively, you can choose a small self-contained fountain unit and simply lay stones around it on the ground.

Planting By its nature, planting in this feature is not really feasible but the pool will be greatly enhanced by appropriate planting around it: if in shade, ferns would be ideal, while small grasses look tremendous in the sun.

Aftercare There is very little to maintain here, but if the feature is in sun, the water may turn green and discolour the pebbles, which will then need the occasional wash. As with other small water features, the water level will require topping up, and the pump removed for winter.

Freestanding water features

Isolated and freestanding water features add great interest to any garden and double as birdbaths. They also let you grow aquatic plants that you may not otherwise have space for, and so add variety to your garden. Any container will do and there are many designs available, like the gunnera "leaf" shown here. Otherwise, Chinese glazed bowls and jars, troughs in stone or metal, and a host of other ideas could stir your imagination – anything that holds water and is frostproof will do.

Best for These features can be placed anywhere. They are effective by themselves, but can also be used to enhance existing water features on patios, for instance, or at the pool side, the end of a rill, or on a rockery.

Construction No special construction is required but, depending on what you choose, think about the availability of electricity if you want to add a fountain. You may also need to consider drainage to cope with overflow from rainfall. Make sure the feature is placed on a firm foundation.

Planting Usually, planting will be minimal but, in any case, you should always choose plants that fit in with the surroundings. In addition, remember that plant roots can exert tremendous force and break a pot if it is too small to accommodate them.

Aftercare Features like the leaf shown will need cleaning every so often. In addition, they will provide an ideal home for mosquito larvae, so should be emptied and refilled every three weeks from late spring to autumn. Any pumps should be removed for the winter.

Placing your water feature

Before deciding on a location for your pool or pond, you need to find the most suitable position in your garden. Getting this right will prevent problems later, so check each factor here to ensure you site your pond well, and that it provides a beautiful feature in years to come.

Locate utility pipes It is important to check the position of all drainage and water pipes, as well as underground telephone and electricity cables around your house, before you settle on the pool site. Keep an open mind as to the exact position for your water feature, because you may not be able to put it where you initially wanted. Most electricity and telephone cables are found in front gardens, and run from the road to your meter in a straight line. In back gardens, lift manhole covers and see which way the drains run – they are also laid in straight lines.

Provide shelter The site you choose must be capable of providing shelter for both plants and wildlife. Water and damp-loving plants with tall stems can be blown over by the wind, while large-leaved plants can be shredded in gusty sites. Wildlife requires sheltered access to water and protection from predators. Neighbouring shrubberies and flower beds provide cover for birds as well as refuges for emerging froglets and insect larvae. Wind can also blow water from a fountain over the pond edge, emptying it quite quickly.

Avoid overhanging trees There are various reasons for not siting a pond under trees. They obscure light from the pond during the growing season (most water plants need plenty of sunlight to thrive). During autumn and winter, falling leaves will need to be removed from the water since their decaying matter is harmful. In addition, the leaves from some trees, such as rhododendrons, yew, and laburnum, are poisonous and kill fish and inhibit insect and amphibian life. If you want a plain and plantless mirror effect, however, then some shade is an advantage.

Check water table levels A high water table can interfere with the installation of a pond. Flexible liners will be pushed upwards, while rigid liners can be subjected to stress. To find out if you have a potential problem, dig a deep hole to the depth of your proposed pond and in the middle of the site, and fill it with water. If the water drains away quickly, you do not have a problem. If the water persists for a day or more, it would be better to build a raised pond.

Dig a hole to the depth of your proposed pond and fill it with water.

If the water drains away quickly, the water table level is low enough for a pond.

Assess the view When choosing the site for your pond, view it from all directions in the garden and also from windows and doorways in the house. One of the most appealing things about water is the reflection on its surface, so to get an idea of the intended effect, lay a large mirror on the site and judge its impact.

Choosing a liner

Your choice of liner depends on a number of factors. In the course of planning your pond, you need to take into account how long you want it to last, its position, the condition of the soil, and the style of pond you want.

Butyl and plastic liners

These come in a wide price range, reflecting quality. Ordinary plastic will last for only three or four years; PVC that has been treated to resist sunlight will last some while longer, and butyl can have a life of 30 years or more.

Keep it simple All these liners allow you to make your pond in any shape you like, but the more complicated, the more expensive it will be. Pond liners are easy to install and repair, but they will also need an underlay in stony ground.

Good for small gardens Because of their flexibility, these liners allow you to take advantage of small, awkward spaces. This is a plus in small town gardens, for instance, or where existing structures exclude other kinds of pond.

Preformed liners

Rigid units made of fibreglass or other plastic materials are available in a large range of designs. When making your choice, check that the pond is deep enough to grow the plants you want.

Big advantages Preformed liners are simple to install and have a long life span. They are also easy to keep clean because the surfaces are smooth. Shelving is already built in, which is a bonus.

Good for formal gardens Preformed pools are particularly useful in formal surroundings, because their rigid structure makes edging with paving or ornamental brickwork a simpler task. They are also useful for making smaller water features in tight spaces.

Concrete liners

The concrete pond has declined in popularity because of problems with the material. Uneven settlement can lead to cracks and frost damage. Concrete ponds are also more time-consuming to install.

The pluses Using concrete lets you plan the shape you want, as well as making it easier to include features like islands, which are more difficult with other liners. These ponds are particularly suited to formal settings.

Long-lasting With proper, skilled construction, taking into account the soil conditions and the possibility of frost damage, you can make a pond that will last virtually for ever. A concrete-lined pool can also be combined with rills and pump housing.

Calculating quantities for liners

Square and rectangular ponds You need to know the length, width, and depth of your pond. To allow for overlap at the edges, add twice the depth (d) plus 45cm (18in) to the length (l), then add twice the depth plus 45cm (18in) to the width (w). Multiply the answers together; ie, (2d + 45cm + l) x (2d + 45cm + w).

Circular pools Here, the size of liner required is the diameter of the pool plus twice the depth, plus 45cm (18in), multiplied by the diameter plus twice the depth plus 45cm (18in).

Irregular pools For simple irregular shapes, measure the maximum width, length, and depth, and use the same formula for square and rectangular pools. If the pool is more complex, break it down into simpler shapes – a square plus a circle, for example – and calculate the quantity needed for each, then add them together.

Making an edge

It is essential that you decide on the edging before you install a pond. It is the last job you do, but can also cause the most problems. Edging hides the plastic lining and makes a good frame.

Pebbles and boulders

If your pool has paving at one or more of its sides, or is bordered by a rockery or a flower bed, then large pebbles and boulders will make excellent edging. They should be sited to prevent soil being washed into the pond as well as to hold the liner edge down firmly. In the initial building phase of the pond, create a dip to seat the stones firmly in place behind the liner and to provide a flat shelf for the smaller stones at the front (on the water side). Planting behind the stones completes the job and helps create a natural appearance, but the edging should not be completely hidden.

This kind of shelved edging allows toads, newts, and frogs free access to the water, as well as offering a convenient means for them to get out again.

Timber and decking

A variety of wooden materials are suitable for edging ponds. If you have a very informal pool bordered largely by flower beds or a bog garden, you can use small tree trunks and old logs laid horizontally. They will prevent soil being washed into the pond by the weather, but because they eventually rot away, they will need replacing.

In more formal situations, timber planks and log-rolls, available from garden centres, make excellent edging materials. Planning ahead is important because all treated wood must be sealed with a silicone sealant to prevent unwanted chemicals leaching into the water.

Timber planks and decks make beautiful poolside patios, and can be raised on brick pillars over the edge of the water. You will need to cover the timber with wire netting, because it can become very slippery in wet weather. Also, use a silicone sealant on brick pillars that will be submerged.

The whole ensemble must be firmly fixed into place and constructed well to avoid tilting and displacement, particularly if it cantilevers out over the water surface. Unless you are a skilled DIYer, you may need to call in professional help to install a raised waterside deck.

A naturalistic edging of pebbles and boulders.

This wooden decking provides a crisp edge.

Lawns and borders

Many ponds are sited either in a lawn or at the edge of a grassed area, where you will want the grass itself to make an edge for the pond.

The best way to create this kind of edging is to cut out three-sided turves around the pond, leaving the back edge attached to the lawn. Roll each turf back so that a row of bricks or blocks can be installed around the actual pond edge to make a firm foundation for the turves when you roll them back towards the water. Without this preparation, you will have difficulty later keeping the edge neatly cut, because the pond water will make the ends of the turves wet, and the mower will gradually push the grass lower and lower until it disappears into the pond.

Alternatively, you can use edging plants, but the same principles hold. You must keep the soil out of the water, preferably using low growing, creeping ground-cover plants. They will grow towards the light, so plant them where they will be drawn to the sun and effectively screen the liner at the edge. Otherwise, they will grow away from the edge you are trying to hide.

Bricks and paving

Hard materials, such as paving slabs, tiles, or bricks, make ideal edging for formal pools and those on patios or in small, enclosed spaces. When choosing materials, be guided by the colour and style of the materials in the existing surroundings.

Edging like this must be constructed properly and needs a good foundation of hardcore to start with, topped with a layer of mortar. Bricks are the most difficult to lay successfully; great care is required in putting them together so that rows look neat. Any extra rows needed to link the construction to an existing bricked area must also fit in correctly. Flagstones are somewhat easier because each covers a larger area, but they are very heavy and need to be cemented in firmly. They should also not stick out over the water more than 8cm (3in) – inevitably, one or two will work loose, and standing on the edge to feed fish can become risky.

When constructing this type of edging, try to ensure that as little cement as possible falls into the water (it is very poisonous to fish). If some does go in accidentally, either change the water or leave it to stand for a month or so before introducing any fish.

Edging plants soften the pond rim.

Brick edging gives a clean finish to a formal pool.

Pond lighting

Lighting brings a water feature to life after dark. You can create many different effects, from illuminating the flow of a fountain or floodlighting an entire pond to floating candles on the surface on a summer's evening.

Choosing your lights

Water feature lights can be submerged in a pond, placed on the water surface, or installed in the garden to throw light on a particular feature, such as a cascade or waterfall. The equipment can be quite obtrusive, particularly during the day, so you may need to consider using rocks, pebbles, and/or plants to conceal it. Pots, jars, and other containers can also hide electrical flexes and other lighting equipment.

Before you install lighting, consider its effect on neighbouring buildings, trees, and shrubs where people or wildlife may be trying to rest. If you have fish, leave parts of your pond unlit so that they can escape the glare. Make sure that your lighting system is connected by a qualified electrician, only use equipment specifically designed for outdoor and underwater use, and always include a circuit breaker. Bury reinforced connecting cables deep enough to avoid disturbing them.

Underwater lights These are submerged just beneath the water surface, and are ideal for informal ponds because they create a relaxed effect. They can also be moved around the pond as required.

Floating candles These are very effective for *al fresco* entertaining on a balmy summer's evening. There are many designs of candle holders to choose from, but you may find that those designed to shelter the flame from the wind are more practical. Also, if the flame isn't protected, there is a danger that it may scorch or set fire to nearby vegetation, or the wax or oil may be blown into the water.

Fixed lights Permanent lights are installed in a fixed position on dry ground in the garden and are best for illuminating features such as ornaments and fountains close to the water's edge. Before buying any equipment, you can get an idea of the effect you want using an ordinary torch. Experiment with different colours and lenses, too, but bear in mind that a garish scheme is often less effective than a low-key, simple arrangement. White lights are usually more restful than coloured ones.

Fibre optics The use of this technology in pond lighting allows you to create attractive fountain effects – even if you don't have a fountain. Fibre optic lights are available in many colours, and can be programmed to perform patterned lighting sequences, both in and out of the water.

Submerged lights highlight the movement of water

Floating candles on still water create a feeling of serenity

Lighting effects

Highlighting You can use lighting to focus on just one or two aspects of a water feature. Here, submerged lamps shine upwards, giving the impression that light is pouring down from the water spouts. The rest of the feature is kept in semi-darkness to accentuate shadows, giving an impression of greater space.

Mirroring The reflective quality of water is one of its main attractions, which is why you don't want to lose this at night. A dual-purpose ornament, such as this circular ring, provides good reflection during the day but really comes into its own at night when lit up to cast a sparkling circular reflection on the water's surface.

Focusing colour Cleverly concealed lighting in different colours softly illuminates this roof garden. The lighting has been installed underneath grilles around the pond and within the peripheral planting to complement the colours of the pond and foliage, and to draw attention to the surrounding landscaping.

Underwater lighting The suffused glow produced by partly or wholly hidden submerged lighting creates an atmosphere of mystery and intrigue. It is achieved easily by a simple, inexpensive lighting kit, and the effect is created as much by the shadows as the well-illuminated area.

What pump where?

The sight and sound of moving water create a magical effect in the garden, but before you choose a fountain or cascade consider what type of pump and filter it will require, and where you should locate them.

Choosing a pump

There are pumps for every purpose and you must be clear about what you want your pump to do. The two main categories are surface pumps, which sit beside the pond, and submersible pumps sited under the water.

When choosing a pump consider the effects you want: a fountain, bubbling pool, watercourse, or a combination of these? Also, what spray shape do you want in your fountain, and how high should the water reach?

Then calculate the volume of your main pond (length x width x depth), and relate this to the flow rate per hour of the pump, which must not be greater than the volume.

Housing surface pumps and filters

Surface pumps can be noisy and are usually set inside a watertight brick box at the side of the pool. The box should include an airbrick for ventilation, a hole at the bottom to allow water to drain out if there is a leak, and a hole in one wall for a large pipe to accommodate an inlet pipe for the pond water and the pump's electrical cable.

The size of the box depends on your pump, but it should be large enough to allow space for adjustments. Cover it with a wooden lid painted with waterproof paint, which you can disguise with planting, as long as it doesn't obstruct access to the pump.

There are two kinds of filter; the best are biological filters containing bacteria that purify the water. Alternatively, mechanical filters simply strain solid particles out of the water. Both types can be fed with water from the pond, either before or after it passes through the pump.

Surface filters should be set at the highest point of a water feature, and the pump positioned as far as possible from where filtered water returns to the pond (ie, in the lower pool of a cascade). This ensures that as much water as possible passes through the filter.

Choosing the right pump will ensure that the water flows at just the right speed through your fountain, cascade, or feature.

Build a brick box for a surface pump, and include an airbrick, a drainage hole, and a hole for a large pipe.

Positioning submersible pumps and filters

The easiest and quietest pump to install is a submersible type. Raise the pump on a few bricks to reduce the amount of sludge passing into the strainer.

The position of the pump depends on whether or not you are using a surface filter. If you are, follow the advice for surface filters, and position it as far away as possible from the point where the filtered water returns to the pond.

However, if you have a submersible filter, it needs to be placed close to the pump on the floor of the pond, because the pump sucks water through the filter. Both the pump and filter should be as close as possible to a fountain or set under a waterfall. This means that the water will have to travel the shortest distance up through the fountain or to the top of the waterfall, ensuring you get the best out of your pump.

Header pools for streams and cascades

If you have chosen a watercourse to simulate a stream flowing into your pond, you will need a small pool at the top of your water feature to act as a reservoir, from which the water can flow down. Known as a header pool, this is usually more effective than simply pumping the water up to discharge from a hose.

Your header pool may be too small to contain fish, but if it is large enough, fix a galvanized grille securely where the water flows down into the stream, to prevent the fish escaping. The grille will slow the rate of water flow, so make allowances for this when choosing your pump.

When installing the hose from the pump to deliver water to a header pool, make sure that the end is above the water level. If it is below the water level in the pool, then the water will be siphoned out when the pump is switched off. Alternatively, you can use a non-return valve to prevent the water from flowing the wrong way down the delivery hose.

Submersible pumps are easy to install and quiet. Place them on a brick or two at the bottom of your pond or pool.

Make a small pool, known as a header pool, above your waterfall or stream to act as a reservoir before the water flows down.

Pumps for different features

Choosing the right pump for the job is very important. Consult your supplier to make sure you buy one that has the power to do what you want it to do.

Simple fountains in ponds

Single or multiple pumps can be used and should be placed well away from water lilies. The fall of water from the fountain should also be clear of the pond edge.

Pump type Use a submersible pump, placed as close to the fountain unit base as possible. If you have more than one unit, place the pump halfway between them.

Ornamental fountains

The range of fountains you can buy is enormous – they come in a wide variety of sizes and designs. When choosing a pump for your water feature, be guided by the style of your pond and garden. You will also need to consider the ease of installation in combination with the pump required.

Pump type A submersible pump of the right calibre is needed. Ask your supplier to help you select a pump that is powerful enough for your fountain design, particularly if you have chosen a combination fountain with multiple spouts. Output must be strong enough to raise the water to the correct height and distribute water evenly over the whole fountain. Large outdoor fountains can also be operated by surface pumps (*see p.40*).

Bubble pools

There are simple or complex forms available, but all are constructed over a concealed reservoir, which must have an easy, if hidden, access point. The reservoir does not have to be very large but if it is not big enough, it will need to be topped up frequently to compensate for water loss through evaporation.

Pump type A submersible pump is sited in the reservoir. If you have one outlet, you will need a fairly small pump, since it only needs to pump the water up a short distance. If you have several outlets, as in this picture, you will need a more powerful pump or three small ones.

Multi-headed fountains

A huge variety of designs is available and in a wide choice of materials. When you are considering which model to buy, remember that the size and reach of the water output of the fountain is part of the design, so choose a multi-headed fountain that suits the scale of your pool.

Pump type Submersible pumps located under the fountain suit this form perfectly. Consider the number of outlets the fountain has and the height of any jets it may be designed to produce. These factors influence the strength of output your pump will need to produce (though this will be adjustable to an extent).

Rills and water channels

Ideal for small gardens, rills and channels offer the sound and sight of running water but take up very little space. Derived originally from Islamic concepts, and brought to fruition in a variety of wonderful Middle Eastern gardens, the idea can be modified and modernized as shown here. Water flows by gravity from a reservoir pool at the highest end and is then recirculated from a sump at the lowest point.

Pump type A submersible pump placed at the lowest point will move the water back to the reservoir. The pump may have to be more powerful than you might think – its capacity will depend on the distance from the end of the rill to the reservoir and the height of the reservoir above the pump, as well as the rate of flow you want to achieve.

Letterbox-style features

This is another useful style to adopt, especially in small gardens. Set up a water trough with a small flat outlet like a letterbox so that moving water flows out over the lip. The water collects in a small pool that acts as a reservoir beneath the letterbox-style outlet, from which it is pumped back up into the trough.

Pump type Again, a submersible pump will do the job very well. Its specifications will depend on the height of the upper level of water and the distance from the pump to the point where the water enters the trough.

Choosing soils and containers

Make sure that your aquatics and bog plants flourish year after year by planting them in suitable soil and choosing appropriate containers.

Soils for pond plants

Good soil promotes plant growth and quickly helps to establish a healthy balance in your pond. It also helps prevent algae from clouding the water. The best growing medium is a well-drained garden soil that has not been contaminated by pesticides. Add some small grit or sand to open it up so that oxygen-carrying water can percolate through it easily. The soil should be slightly on the acid side or neutral (avoid chalky soil). Or use topsoil from the garden centre mixed with well-rotted manure. Artificial aquatic soils are convenient but not as good as garden soil in the long run.

Clay in your soil can turn the water milky. To solve this problem, put some well-rotted manure into a plastic bag. Tie the opening, perforate the bag with a kitchen fork and place it in the water for a week or so. This will clear the water by increasing the acidity and coagulating the clay.

Soils for bog gardens

A stagnant bog contains little or no oxygen and is useless for growing most bog plants. To establish a successful bog garden, make sure that the bog is well drained by piercing holes in the liner to prevent waterlogging and ensure that plenty of oxygen reaches the plant roots. To aid this process, choose a permeable loam, which can be made by mixing small grit and some sand with your soil, breaking up any lumps of clay at the same time.

Just like plants in a flower bed, bog plants need feeding well and so you should include well-rotted manure in your mix, too. Be prepared to fork in more manure in subsequent years.

If your soil is very sandy and free-draining, it may lose moisture too quickly. In this case, dig in lots of well-rotted manure and some clay, available from landscaping suppliers, to improve water retention.

The best growing medium for aquatics is free-draining garden soil that is free from pesticides.

Unless your soil is very sandy, bog gardens should be filled with garden soil mixed with grit and some sand.

Aquatic basket options

The visual effect obtained with planting baskets will never be quite the same as when you grow your plants in a natural layer of soil. However, using baskets does have several advantages. First of all, since many water plants can be very invasive, baskets enable you to keep them under control. They also allow you to move the plants about as desired. And finally, when the time comes to divide your plants, baskets make the process much easier.

Plastic baskets are available in every possible shape and size, to fit every situation. They have an open lattice construction that allows all-important oxygen to reach the plant roots. It is best to choose baskets with a fine meshed lattice that don't need lining with hessian or plastic netting. Baskets with larger mesh require lining to prevent the soil leaking out of the holes. Hessian, in particular, quickly rots and needs continual replacement, so if your baskets do have the larger mesh size, line them with fine plastic netting instead.

When choosing an aquatic basket, also consider the eventual size of the plant that is going to live in it. Too small a basket will restrict its growth, as well as making the planting unstable and prone to falling over.

Alternative container ideas

There are other containers that fulfil the same specifications as rigid plastic baskets. For instance, floppy, fine-netted bags can be used instead.

Earthenware jars and bowls with holes in the sides are particularly useful in small water features. They will usually need to be lined with plastic netting, but support plants successfully and are features in their own right.

Strawberry planters can look very attractive when combined with a small spout. Place the pot in a reservoir of water or at the edge of a pond, and feed a hose attached to a small pump up through the hole at the bottom. Fill the pot with soil and plant small aquatics so they grow out of the holes. The water will trickle down through the planter and emerge at the plant openings or, if the water pressure is a little higher, it will spill over the sides of the pot, too. Such an arrangement provides height, as well as allowing you to grow a number of small marginal aquatics where you can see and appreciate them easily.

Where there is very little room, attractive features can be made from a series of stepped containers, mounted on walls for instance. Water spills from one to another.

Choose an aquatic basket with fine-meshed lattice that does not need lining.

Flexible aquatic bags are useful for ponds with uneven shelves or bottoms because they mould to the surface.

Creating
small features

Water-filled bowls and barrels can be squeezed into the tiniest of courtyards, while a bubble pool will add a dynamic feature to a patio or pebble garden. In this chapter, step-by-step sequences show you how to make these features, as well as a simple raised pool and wall fountain. Remember that if your feature needs an outdoor electricity supply, you must by law employ a qualified electrician to install it for you.

Create a container pool

Quick and easy to make, this glazed container pool is perfect for tiny patios, balconies, and roof terraces. Plant with a miniature water lily and small aquatic plants like *Juncus effusus* f. *spiralis*.

Tip for success

Water lilies need a sunny site in order to flower well. Put them on the bottom of your pool, and don't overfeed.

1 Choose a bowl-shaped ceramic container in a colour that you like. It should be as wide at the top as possible, and about 45cm (18in) deep. Make sure that it is frostproof, otherwise it will crack when temperatures drop.

2 Clean the inside of the pot with a stiff brush and rinse with fresh water – don't use soap or detergent. Waterproof unglazed pots with a urethane spray or neoprene paint. Use wine corks to plug drainage holes.

3 Fill the container with water to about 5cm (2in) below the rim – rainwater is best but if this is not possible, use ordinary tap water, provided that you leave the container to stand for a day or so before planting.

4 Choose an aquatic plant basket with small holes in the sides. Line baskets with large holes with plastic netting, not hessian, to prevent soil from leaking out. Put a layer of good loam or loam-based compost in the basket.

Create a container pool *continued*

5 Carefully remove the water lily from its original container. Position the lily in the centre of the aquatic basket, then start pouring in either untreated garden soil or loam-based compost around the plant.

6 Gently firm in the soil. Inspect the plant and remove any duckweed or algae on the leaves by wiping gently with a cloth. Make sure that the leaves don't dry out during this preparation by spraying them with water.

7 If you wish, you can stabilize the surface of the soil by covering it with a layer of pea-gravel. Wash the gravel well in several rinses of water beforehand in order to remove any dust and impurities.

Tip for success

If the container is too deep for your plants, place a layer of bricks in the bottom to bring them up to the right level.

8 Place the planted basket in the prepared container. Don't worry if the leaves are submerged, they will reach the surface very quickly. You can then add one or two other small aquatic plants in separate pots.

Construct a rustic barrel pool

Wooden half-barrels make perfect mini water features. You can be quite ambitious with your planting (marsh marigold, *Sagittaria*, and *Butomus* adorn this barrel) and even add a fish or two.

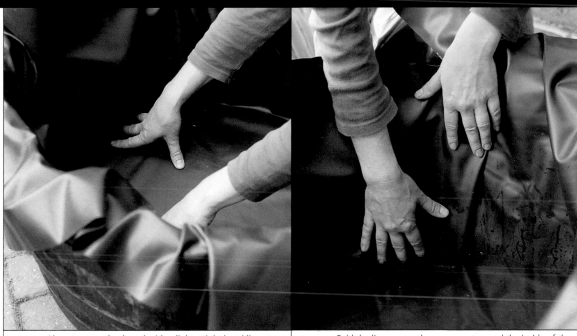

1 Line your wooden barrel with a lightweight butyl liner to make it waterproof. The liner will also prevent poisonous preservatives in the wood from leaching into the water, damaging plants and fish.

2 Fold the liner as neatly as you can around the inside of the barrel. Flatten any creases and press firmly into and over the base of the barrel, to create a smooth surface. Half-fill the barrel with water to push the liner down further.

3 Using a pair of scissors (most kitchen scissors will do the job), cut off most of the excess liner, leaving an edge of about 3in (7.5cm) above the rim of the barrel.

4 Fold down the top edge of the liner and tack it to the inside of the barrel just under the rim. Use short galvanized tacks that don't penetrate right through the wood.

Construct a rustic barrel pool *continued*

5 Note the different planting depths of the plants you have chosen – this is the distance from the top of the planting basket to the water surface – and arrange bricks in the bottom of the barrel to accommodate them.

6 Place soil into the baskets and then add your plants. If you can, use baskets with small holes because those with larger holes will need to be lined with fine plastic netting to prevent soil from leaking into the water.

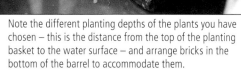

7 Oxygenators, which are usually bought as cuttings, can be dibbled in with a pencil. Keep them close to the surface when you first plant them, so that they receive as much light as possible. Lower them when they are growing well.

8 To prevent soil from muddying the water, cover each planted basket surface with a layer of gravel. This also prevents fish from disturbing the soil if you plan to keep one or two in your barrel.

9   Place the planted baskets into the barrel, making sure that each plant is at its required depth (a few centimetres deeper or shallower will do no harm). Fill the barrel with water slowly, so as not to disturb the plants.

Make a beautiful bubble pool

A bubble pool, with its mesmerizing sounds and patterns created by the gently moving water, is one of the most desirable water features you can make, and fits even the smallest of gardens.

1 Dig a hole bigger than the size of the water reservoir that will be positioned below the bubble pool. Consult a qualified electrician to install a waterproof electricity supply to the location for the pump.

2 Protecting your hands with thick gloves, remove any sharp stones and edge the hole with damp sand. Install the water reservoir, making sure it is level by using a spirit level placed in three or four positions.

3 Pack the area around the reservoir with more sand or other similar material. When the reservoir is firmly in position, check once again that it is level using a spirit level – this is very important.

Make a beautiful bubble pool *continued*

4   Once the reservoir is level, place the pump into the reservoir so that the exit pipe will reach through the hole in the bottom of the terracotta pot. You may need an extension tube for this. Place the lid over the reservoir.

5   Place the terracotta pot over the reservoir with the pump pipe protruding up through the hole in the base. Seal the pump pipe into place with silicone sealant and leave to dry and harden thoroughly for 24 hours.

6   Attach a long section of delivery piping to the water flow adjuster. Then attach the delivery pipe and flow adjuster to the pump tube at the base of the pot. The delivery pipe should reach just under the rim of the pot.

7   Fill both the reservoir and the terracotta pot with a garden hose. The water level should be just under the top of the delivery pipe.

8 The electrical flex must be protected by special piping – a qualified electrician will advise you on this and will install an outdoor electricity supply. Ensure all electrical connections are fitted with an RCD circuit-breaker.

9 Conceal the plastic edge of the reservoir with gravel, leaving a small gap clear for topping up the water. In warm weather, when evaporation rates increase, you will need to top up the water at least once a week.

10 Larger pebbles, rocks, or whatever you choose can also be placed over the gravel around the base of the container. Switch on the pump and adjust the flow so the water bubbles over the top of the pot and down the sides.

Make a raised bed water feature

The water from this steel wall fountain flows into a Belfast sink set in a raised bed. The edge of the feature doubles as a seat, and it is ideal for a small space, such as a patio.

1 Measure the area for the raised bed. For the frame, lay four battens of treated timber 5x5cm (2x2in) in position on the ground. Fix together with galvanized screws. Attach the four vertical posts with screws at a 45° angle.

2 Secure the tops of the vertical posts to four horizontal posts with galvanized screws. Position the frame snugly against the wall to provide support for the bed.

3 Screw three planks to the front and sides of the vertical posts. Leave a gap of 8cm (3in) between the planks. The bed will be lined with black plastic, which will show through the gaps, so add more planks if you want to hide it.

4 Use a staple gun to fix strong, heavy-gauge black plastic sheeting securely to the inside of the frame (not against the wall). Paint the inside of the bed where it has not been covered by plastic with outdoor paint.

Make a raised bed water feature *continued*

5 Check the height of the Belfast sink in the raised bed. If it is too low, use concrete blocks or bricks to bring it up to the correct height. (If you are not using a sink as the water container, line the entire bed with plastic.)

6 To make the sink watertight, cut a piece of waterproofed wood to fit the drain area of the sink exactly. Paint it and glue it into position with waterproof silicone. Run silicone around the edge for a completely watertight seal.

7 Place the sink onto the concrete blocks, positioning it in the centre of the raised bed. Make sure that the sink is absolutely level using a spirit level.

8 If you have room for plants on either side of the sink, pour gravel or pebbles into the gaps up to a third of the depth of the sink. This will provide drainage when the beds are planted up.

9 Fill the gaps with soil or a multi-purpose compost. Tamp it down gently and then top up. Fix planks of wood on top of the frame, on each side and at the front. Cut the corners at a 45° angle and screw into position.

10 Paint the front of the raised bed with outdoor wood paint or wood preservative in a colour that contrasts well with the black lining and your plants.

11 Remove the plants from their pots and plant them in the compost. If you are going to add a fountain, choose damp-loving plants, such as grasses or ferns, since they will be subjected to water spray.

12 If you are not going to add a fountain, this is the last step. Fill the sink with water, and make sure the soil in the beds is kept moist at all times by watering it as necessary. To incorporate a wall fountain, see p.64 overleaf.

Make a raised bed water feature *continued*

13 Before installing the wall fountain, buy a pump capable of pumping water from the bottom of the sink to the height of your proposed fountain head. Cut a transparent plastic pipe to the height of the fountain and fix it to the pump.

14 Place the pump in the sink and run the cable along the back of the sink to an outdoor electrical point (installed by a qualified electrician). Run water through the pump to check that it is working before attaching the fountain.

15 Attach the other end of the plastic pipe to the base of the fountain's water reservoir with a butterfly clip and tighten the clip with a scewdriver.

16 Fit the reservoir and water chute to the wall by drilling holes with a masonry drill bit and fixing them with rawlplugs and galvanized screws. Add rubber washers under the screw heads to prevent any leakage.

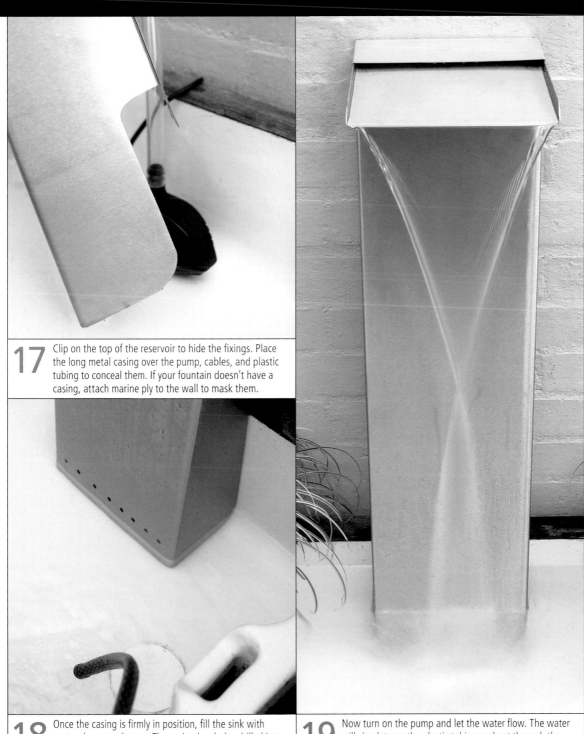

17 Clip on the top of the reservoir to hide the fixings. Place the long metal casing over the pump, cables, and plastic tubing to conceal them. If your fountain doesn't have a casing, attach marine ply to the wall to mask them.

18 Once the casing is firmly in position, fill the sink with water almost to the top. The casing has holes drilled into the base so the water can reach the pump.

19 Now turn on the pump and let the water flow. The water will circulate up the plastic tubing and out through the top of the feature. The lip of the chute is tilted slightly downwards for a better flow.

Create a rill

The crisp lines of a rill make it an ideal water feature for a contemporary garden. Easy to construct, this brick-edged rill is set off by banks of slate and decorative pebbles.

1 Rake the surface of the soil to level it. If your rill is to run through a lawn, cut out the required amount of turf to expose the soil. Mark out the exact length and width of your rill with pegs and string.

2 Using your string as a guide, dig out the central channel of the rill to a depth of 15–20cm (6–8in). Create shallower shelves on either side for the brick edging (*see p.68*). Use a spirit level to check that the top of the rill is level.

3 Line the base of the channel with a layer of soft sand and compact it down until firm with a piece of wood. Use a spirit level to check that the base is level.

Create a rill *continued*

4 At one end of the rill, dig a hole for the reservoir tank, deep enough for the rim of the tank to sit level with the base of the rill. Place the tank in the hole, filling in any gaps around the tank with soil.

5 Line the rill with a piece of heavy-duty plastic liner wide enough to provide an overlap of 20cm (8in) on either side that will sit under the edging of bricks. Press the liner into the trench firmly, smoothing out creases and folds.

6 Edge the rill with bricks on both sides and at the end opposite the reservoir. Use a ready-mixed mortar about 5cm (2in) thick to bed the bricks, and keep it out of the rill. Mortar between the bricks, leaving a gap at the top.

7 Cut a piece of flexible pipe that measures the length of the rill plus 45cm (18in). Lay out the pipe along one side of the rill. Place the pump in the reservoir tank. Run the electric cable through a conduit to an outdoor socket.

8 Fit one end of the flexible pipe to the pump, check that the pipe runs the full length of the feature, and then trim any excess with a sharp knife. Test that the pump is working and adjust it to give you the correct flow of water.

9 Place a wire mesh grille over the reservoir tank containing the pump, and disguise it with carefully positioned slabs or pebbles. Keep the arrangement simple so that you can service the pump easily.

10 Cover the flexible pipe and the bottom of the rill with slate or pebbles to hide both the plastic liner and the pipe. Fill the rill channel with water and switch on the pump. Use a decorative aggregate as an edging.

Building ponds and cascades

A lushly planted naturalistic pond adds a dramatic focal point to a small garden, yet despite appearances, it is quite easy to build. Discover how by following the step-by-step sequences in this chapter. Plant lovers may like to edge their pool with a bog garden, which is also simple to make. Building a cascade or waterfall is more challenging, but the final effect makes it well worth the effort. Find out how to create a cascade in your garden at the end of the chapter.

Build an informal pond

The advantage of making a butyl-lined pond is that it can be any shape you want. Remember, though, that the more complicated the design, the more expensive the pond will be.

1 Calculate roughly what size of liner you can afford and estimate the eventual pond size (*see p.35*). Lay out the shape of the pond with a garden hose, which will help you to achieve a smooth, curved outline.

2 Dig out the whole area to a depth of 45cm (18in), dumping the spoil well away from the edges. Gently angle the edges if the soil is light and crumbly; if the ground is firm, make them more vertical.

3 Excavate the central, deeper part of the pond, leaving a shelf 30–45cm (12–18in) wide around the outer edges. Make part of the central excavation 75cm (30in) deep and part 1m (3ft) deep.

Build an informal pond *continued*

4 It is very important to make sure that the top edges of the pond are level all around. Build up or dig them out to achieve this. Place a spirit level on a straight plank, and test it in six or seven places around the perimeter.

5 Remove sharp stones in the walls and floor. Line a small pond with pieces of carpet or newspapers; larger ponds need proper underlay. Don't use sand because it can fall off the sides and fill up the hole.

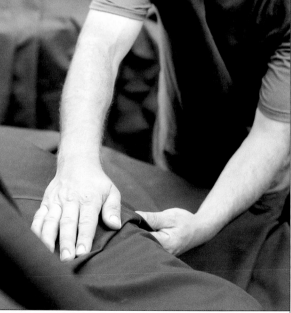

6 Centre the liner over the hole and push the middle down a little, allowing pleats to form against the sides and various levels. Fill the deepest part of the hole with water, which will hold the liner in place and drag more of it down.

7 Finish folding the liner over the shelf and top edge; make small adjustments by gently pulling the liner. Make sure the liner is well bedded into the bottom of the pond. If it is not, you will have to siphon out the water and start again.

Once the pond is filled, trim the liner with a Stanley knife or sharp scissors, leaving up to 45cm (18in) excess around the edge.

8 Resume filling the pond with water. The weight of the water will force the liner hard against the inside walls and shelving. Try not to stand still on surplus liner because this will prevent it from being pulled into the pond.

Build an informal pond *continued*

9 The edges can be turfed, in which case you need only 23cm (9in) of excess liner; for a paved or rocky edge you will need more. Paving stones and rocks can be mortared onto the liner, but ensure no mortar falls into the water.

10 When placing paving stones or rocks in position, make sure that you do not let them overhang the water by more than about 5cm (2in). This prevents them tipping up and falling into the pond when the inner edges are walked on.

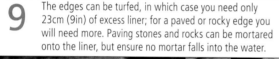

11 When placing decorative rocks in the water, make sure the liner is protected by placing the rocks on folded plastic sacks. For a natural effect, position the rocks so that the strata lines all run in the same direction.

12 Start planting deep-water aquatic plants in their baskets, lowering them to the appropriate depths. Remember that the planting depth is measured from the top of the basket to the water surface.

13 Place marginal plants on the shelving, with taller plants at the back of the pond so they don't obscure the water. Position all the plants in groups with spaces between them to achieve a natural appearance.

Make a flowering bog garden

This feature allows you to grow different kinds of moisture-loving plants beside your pond if the soil is naturally dry. Brighten up your bog garden with flowers such as primulas, irises, and arum lilies.

1 Lay out a flexible garden hose on the ground (a bog garden looks particularly good alongside a pond) in the desired shape. Dig out the area to a depth of at least 60cm (24in), to accommodate the roots of the plants.

2 Put the liner in as before when building the pond (*see p.74*), but use your hands to get the liner into place, not water. It is a good idea to stabilize excess liner with bricks, moving them out as you push the liner into the hole.

3 It is essential to provide drainage in this kind of bog garden, otherwise the soil will quickly lose oxygen and turn sour, and nothing will grow. Perforate the liner with a fork in several places across the base only.

4 To prevent the soil from clogging up the holes, put a layer of stones 8cm (3in) deep on the bottom (this is the same principle as putting crocks in a flowerpot). Fill with good garden soil over a layer of well-rotted compost.

Make a flowering bog garden *continued*

Tip for success

To make topping up easier, coil a length of leaky pipe around the bog garden, and attach to a connector for a garden hose.

5 Trim the edge of the liner and cover with turf or stone, as preferred. The bog garden will lose moisture through evaporation and need topping up occasionally, but it will retain rainwater longer than the rest of the garden.

6 Place a perforated hose around the perimeter of the bog garden. Prepare the soil for planting by plugging in your garden hose to the connector on the perforated hose. Leave the tap running until the surface is quite wet.

7 Check how big your bog plants will grow and space them out accordingly on the soil. When you are happy with the planting scheme, dig planting holes. Tip each plant out of its pot and gently spread out its roots. Start planting.

8 Position the crown of each plant just above soil level, and firm down the earth. Plants like the ligularia shown here can be planted where they will get some breeze, to reveal the wonderful colour on the undersides of their leaves.

Build a pond with a rigid liner

One of the easiest ways to create a
pond is to use a rigid, preformed liner.
Choose one that is deep enough for
the plants you want, and install it with
the shelves at the back so the water
can be seen in the foreground.

1 Place the liner in position. Push bamboo canes in the soil at intervals around the liner to mark its outline. Carefully remove the liner. Wind string or rope around the canes to show the precise shape of the liner.

2 Dig out the soil according to the outline but adding an extra 15cm (6in) all around. Remove any large stones and roots as you go. Save the excavated soil on a plastic sheet for use elsewhere in the garden.

3 Using a plank and a spirit level, check in several places that the entire site is level. It is important to be thorough at this stage, otherwise you risk having a pond with an uneven water level.

4 Line the bottom of the hole with soft sand, newspapers, or old carpet to a depth that brings the top of the liner level with the edges of the hole. Compact the material well to prevent the liner from moving when filled.

Build a pond with a rigid liner *continued*

5   Lower the liner into position. Use a spirit level on a plank of wood again to check that it is level. You may need to remove the liner several times and adjust the materials underneath to achieve this.

6   Fill the liner to three-quarters full with water. Rainwater is best but you can also use tap water, provided you leave it to stand for a week before adding any fish.

7   Pack sand or soil down the sides of the liner to fix it securely into place. The drier the sand or soil, the easier this job will be. Then top up the water level to about 10cm (4in) from the rim of the liner.

8   Fix an edging, such as slates or cobbles, in place. You can use mortar but be careful not to drop any into the water. Alternatively, firm the stones into the surrounding soil far enough back so they won't topple into the pond.

Tip for success

Always check that new plants are disease free before planting. Cut out dead foliage, and remove obvious pests, such as snails.

9 Check the planting depths for your chosen plants and move your containers into place, positioning taller plants at the back. If you plan to keep fish, make sure that you cover the soil in the baskets with pebbles.

Create a butyl-lined cascade

If you have a sloping garden, why not create a stream that cascades into an ornamental pool? If you don't already have a pool, see our step-by-step guides on how to build one (*pp.72–77 and 82–85*).

Tip for success

Create a natural-looking stream by covering the liner with a mixture of stones and gravel. Then soften the margins with a range of moisture-loving plants.

1 Using canes or stakes, mark out the course of the stream and an area for the header pool (*see p.41*) to feed the stream. Dig a trench along the course, and dig the header pool so that it slopes backwards and is deeper at the far end.

2 Measure the water course and buy sufficient butyl liner to cover it, ensuring a generous overlap either side of the stream to allow for the weight of the water. Lay one end of the liner over the edge of the lower pool.

3 Position a large, flat-bottomed stone on the shelf or base of the lower pool at the outlet of the stream, and on top of the stream's butyl liner. If the stone doesn't have a flat base, drain the pond and mortar it in place.

4 To secure the foundation stone, pack stiff mortar between the stone and liner. Roll up the liner and pack more mortar between it and the bank. This will anchor the liner between the mortar wedges. Don't let mortar fall into the water.

Create a butyl-lined cascade *continued*

5 Partially unroll the liner. Place a large stone with a flat top (spill stone) on top of the foundation stone, overlapping it slightly. With a can or hose, check that the water flows smoothly over the spill stone, then mortar it into position.

6 Stack rocks each side of, and higher than, the spill stone, creating a central channel for water to flow through. Test the water flow again and mortar the first layer of stones to the liner. Then cement the remaining stones in place.

7 To prevent water from seeping under the spill stone, pull the liner level with the top of it and pleat the liner. Place another rock behind the liner and spill stone. Secure the liner in place with mortar.

8 Unroll the rest of the liner over the channel and header pool. Mortar another spill stone at the header pool outlet. Check that the stream walls become gradually higher. Mortar more rocks along the edges of the stream and header pool.

9 Place a submersible pump in the lower pond. Take the pipe up one side of the stream to the top of the header pool. Use a stone to disguise the pipe where it enters the pool and bury the delivery pipe. Switch on the pump.

Planting ideas

Aquatic and moisture-loving plants bring water features or bog gardens to life, injecting colour, texture and form. Make the most of these plants by following the inspiring planting recipes in this chapter. The symbols below indicate the conditions each of the plants prefers.

Key to plant symbols

  ♖   Plants given the RHS Award
of Garden Merit

Soil preference

  ◇   Well-drained soil

  ◉   Moist soil

  ●   Wet soil

Preference for sun or shade

  ☀   Full sun

  ☀   Partial or dappled shade

  ☀   Full shade

Hardiness ratings

  ❄   Plants that need protection from frost
over winter

  ❄❄   Plants that survive outside in mild
regions or sheltered sites

  ❄❄❄ Fully hardy plants

  ❄   Tender plants that do not tolerate any
degree of frost

Plant lovers' informal pool

The informal pool is a natural garden feature and the planting should reflect this. It is the sort of pool that a plant lover can revel in because lots of different kinds of plants can be used. Some restraint is called for, though, because the water itself should be the main focus, so try not to obscure it with too many plants. The informal pool forms an integral part of a garden and, for this reason, it can be used to enhance a rockery, the base of a wall, a shrubbery, or herbaceous border.

Border basics

Size 3x3m (10x10ft)

Suits Any garden

Soil Any soil, neutral to acid preferred

Site In full sun or a little shade

Shopping list

- 3 x *Iris ensata*
- 1 x *Miscanthus sinensis* 'Silberfeder'
- 1 x *Nymphaea* 'Escarboucle'
- 3 x *Veronica beccabunga*
- 7 x *Myosotis scorpioides*
- 3 x *Alchemilla mollis*

Planting and aftercare

Most of the planting forms a background to the water. If a bog garden has been made, so much the better, because a huge range of damp-loving plants can be grown. If this is not possible, use plants that like drier conditions instead, such as yellow-flowered *Alchemilla mollis*. Damp-loving plants generally have lacy, lush, or grassy shapes, and any herbaceous plants with similar foliage fit in well.

In either case, choose plants whose size will enable them to grow happily together. After planting, feed the plants regularly: in spring for the pond plants, and in either spring or autumn for the out-of-pond areas. In the autumn, dying foliage and stems should be cleared away and composted.

Iris ensata
❋ ❋ ☼

Miscanthus sinensis 'Silberfeder'
❋ ❋ ❋ ☼ ◐ ♀

phaea 'Escarboucle'

Veronica beccabunga

Myosotis scorpioides

Classical water feature

A small site can be exploited to make a decorative feature, as this classical water spout demonstrates. Here, the lion's head spout is in half-shade and so the main planting consists of ferns and hostas. Together they create interesting contrasts, and some additional colour is provided by the variegated hostas. As long as the site gets the sun for a third of the day, a water iris will successfully inject a strong vertical presence in the spring and summer, and its blue flowers suit the overall scheme.

Water feature basics

Size 2x2m (6x6ft) – the plants could also be kept in containers

Suits A patio edge or a difficult corner

Soil Good neutral to acid loam

Site Half-shade

Shopping list

- 2 x *Dryopteris filix-mas*
- 1 x *Hosta* (*montana*) 'Aureomarginata'
- 1 x *Hosta* 'Gold Standard'
- 1 x *Hosta plantaginea*
- 1 x *Asplenium scolopendrium*
- 1 x *Iris laevigata* (optional)

Planting and aftercare

Fill the bed or containers with a good neutral to acid loam (or loam-based compost). Where the hostas are to be planted, fork in some good well-rotted farm manure. The ferns don't like too much feeding, however. Plant the iris in loam in an aquatic basket. Hostas are prone to attacks from slugs, but if the plants are well fed and growing vigorously, the damage will be reduced. Nevertheless, you can spread slug pellets over the crowns in spring and then mulch thinly over the top, which will feed the plants and prevent birds picking up the pellets. In the autumn, remove dead foliage as the leaves die back. The ferns will last longer than the hostas.

Dryopteris filix-mas
❄❄❄ ◗ ☼ ℣

Hosta (*montana*) 'Aureomarginata'
❄❄❄ ◗ ☼

Hosta 'Gold Standard'
❄❄❄ ◗ ☼

Hosta plantaginea
❄❄❄ ◗ ☼ ☀

Asplenium scolopendrium
❄❄❄ ◗ ◊ ☼ ℣

Additional plant idea

Iris laevigata
❄❄❄ ☼ ℣

Contemporary water lily pond

Modern materials, such as wooden decking, can look good in any setting. Plantings will break up straight, hard lines, and the plants chosen should make vertical as well as horizontal accents. Leaves usually last longer than flowers, so it is best to select plants with contrasting foliage shapes. Choosing plants with different flowering times can also extend the season of interest.

Check the eventual size of each water lily: too small and they will look insignificant; too large and they may take over and obscure the water.

Water feature basics

Size 3x4m (10x12ft)

Suits Small gardens

Soil Good loam throughout

Site An informal sunny position

Shopping list

- 2 x *Nymphaea* 'René Gérard'
- 1 x *Nymphaea* 'Marliacea Chromatella'
- 1 x *Pontederia cordata*
- 3 x *Sagittaria sagittifolia*
- 2 x *Equisetum hyemale*
- 3 x *Ranunculus flammula*

Planting and aftercare

Fill the aquatic baskets, which must be big enough for strong root growth, with good free-draining garden soil. Plant in mid-spring. The water lilies should be placed at the correct depth (the planting depth is the distance from the crown to the surface, not from the basket base).

As the season progresses, remove any dead foliage and flowers. The following spring, divide any plants that have outgrown their baskets and replant. The water lilies should not need to be disturbed for three years or so, when lengths of healthy rhizome with strong terminal buds and roots can be cut out and repotted.

Nymphaea 'René Gérard'
✳✳✳ ☼

Nymphaea 'Marliacea Chromatella'
✳✳✳ ☼ ♈

Pontederia cordata
✳✳✳ ☼ ♈

Sagittaria sagittifolia
✳✳✳ ☼

Equisetum hyemale
✳✳✳ ☼

Additional plant idea

Ranunculus flammula
✳✳✳ ☼

Modern wildlife pond

There is no reason why modern settings and materials can't be used to make a water feature that not only looks up to date, but also fulfils all the criteria for attracting and supporting wildlife. All ponds are really wildlife ponds. Water contained and edged as shown here will attract a wide range of native insects; and many amphibians and other creatures will be able to find a home among the planting, provided they can get in and out of the water easily.

Water feature basics

Size 4x5m (12x15ft)

Suits Large to small gardens

Soil Neutral to acid loam

Site Full sun to half-shade

Shopping list

- 1 x *Iris pseudacorus*
- 1 x *Hosta* 'Sum and Substance'
- 2 x *Angelica archangelica*
- 5 x *Primula pulverulenta*
- 3 x *Lychnis flos-cuculi*
- 1 x *Aponogeton distachyos*

Planting and aftercare

The plants assembled here are all damp lovers and need to grow in well-drained but moist conditions. Most flower in late spring and early summer. There are plenty of them to provide cover for wildlife and nectar to feed insects. The yellow irises and the lychnis will need to be deadheaded because they seed profusely and can spread uncontrollably in later years. The angelica will die after flowering, so you should collect its seed for sowing the following spring for flowers the year after (they are biennials and will produce only leaves in the first year). The primulas can be propagated by division, but you will acquire more plants if you collect their seed, too. Sow the seed in trays indoors in late winter.

Iris pseudacorus
❋❋❋ ☼ ◑ ♈

Hosta 'Sum and Substance'
❋❋❋ ◐ ◑ ♈

Angelica archangelica
❋❋❋ ◐ ☼ ◑

Primula pulverulenta
❋❋ ◑ ♈

Lychnis flos-cuculi
❋❋❋ ◐ ◌ ☼ ◑

Aponogeton distachyos
❋❋❋ ☼ ◑ ◑

Eastern influences

Oriental ideas have been very influential in the design of water features and their associated plantings. Here, the cane fencing, the shape, position, and style of the decking, and the stepping stones all echo eastern ideas. The bulk of the planting consists of grasses, while contrasts in form and texture are provided by the huge leaves of the *Gunnera* and the rounded water lily foliage.

Water feature basics

Size   5x4m (15x12ft)

Suits   Small to medium-sized gardens

Soil   A good rich loam

Site   Sheltered, in full sun

Shopping list

- 3 x *Cyperus involucratus*
- 1 x *Gunnera manicata*
- 2 x *Nymphaea* 'James Brydon'
- 1 x *Lythrum salicaria*
- 3 x *Phragmites australis* or *Butomus umbellatus*

Planting and aftercare

The planting in the water is very simple, allowing only enough water coverage to keep down algae and support some decorative planting. This is why the small water lily *Nymphaea* 'James Brydon' has been chosen; its double, deep pink flowers are also perfectly in keeping with the scheme. It is important to keep the water lilies in check so that there is enough clear water visible to show off the reflections of the grasses. Make sure the *Phragmites australis* is safely contained, otherwise it will take over the whole pool. It is one of the most beautiful grasses you can grow, so it is worth the effort. Deadhead the *Lythrum*, and remove dead leaves and stems before they fall into the water. The *Cyperus* is tender, so bring it into a frost-free place in the winter.

Cyperus involucratus

Gunnera manicata

Nymphaea 'James Brydon'

Lythrum salicaria

Phragmites australis

Alternative plant idea

Butomus umbellatus

Elegant fish pond

One of the main reasons why people build a pond is because they want to enjoy the movement and colour provided by fish. The disadvantages of keeping fish can be mitigated by helpful planting. Although fish excreta contaminate the water, vigorous and greedy plants can reduce any impact. In this arrangement, the bulrush (*Typha*), *Sagittaria*, and *Alisma* are all very beneficial and, provided you don't overfeed the fish, these plants will take up the contaminants.

Water feature basics

Size 3x4m (10x12ft)

Suits Small to medium-sized gardens

Soil Good natural loam

Site Full sun

Shopping list

- 1 x *Typha latifolia*
- 1 x *Ligularia* 'The Rocket'
- 1 x *Ligularia dentata* 'Desdemona'
- 3 x *Sagittaria sagittifolia*
- 1 x *Alisma plantago-aquatica*
- 1 x *Darmera peltata*

Planting and aftercare

Keep the water plants in containers full of good garden soil with some clay. If you want koi carp, remember that they will eat most, if not all, of the submerged plant material. To prevent this, the plants in the water can be fenced off with plastic-covered chicken wire, which should stretch from the bottom of the pond to just under the water surface. The area surrounding this pond is planted with damp-loving varieties to maintain the theme. You will therefore need to keep the soil moist by digging in plenty of well-rotted compost or manure before planting, keeping the soil well watered, and applying a mulch of compost each spring.

Typha latifolia
✿✿✿ ☼

Ligularia 'The Rocket'
✿✿✿ ☼ ◑ ☼ ♔

Ligularia dentata 'Desdemona'
✿✿✿ ☼ ◑ ♔

Sagittaria sagittifolia
✿✿✿ ☼

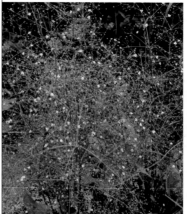

Alisma plantago-aquatica
✿✿✿ ☼ ◑

Darmera peltata
✿✿✿ ☼ ◑ ♔

Colourful water barrels

If you don't want a pond, haven't got room for one, or would like an aquatic patio feature, you can grow water plants in containers. The advantages are that you can see more of the plants than if they were in a pond, and you can move them around the garden. Pots also allow you to display plants in ways that may be difficult to achieve in a pool. For example, trollius look their best when set in a position where the flowers are caught in the light of the setting sun.

Container basics

Size Containers of any size, to suit

Suits Small gardens and patios

Soil Good loam

Site Sun, or partial shade for some

Shopping list

- 2 x *Iris sibirica* 'Perry's Blue'
- 3 x *Trollius chinensis*
- 3 x *Schoenoplectus lacustris* subsp. *tabernaemontani* 'Albescens'
- 3 x *Trollius x cultorum*

Planting and aftercare

Make sure your containers are waterproof, or line them with plastic, and put your plants into aquatic baskets filled with a good loam-based compost before placing them in the water. Planting in baskets makes it easier to position the plants in the container, and more straightforward to lift them later for dividing. Covering the compost with pebbles helps to keep the soil in place when you move the baskets. Keep the containers topped up regularly – you will be surprised at just how much water the plants use. You need to do very little to the plants during the growing season, but when they have finished flowering, you can replace them with others that flower later. Plants in containers are more prone to winter frosts, so give them some protection.

Iris sibirica 'Perry's Blue'
❄❄ ☼

Trollius chinensis
❄❄❄ ☼ ◐

Schoenoplectus lacustris subsp. *tabernaemontani* 'Albescens' ❄❄ ☼

Trollius x cultorum
❄❄❄ ☼ ◐

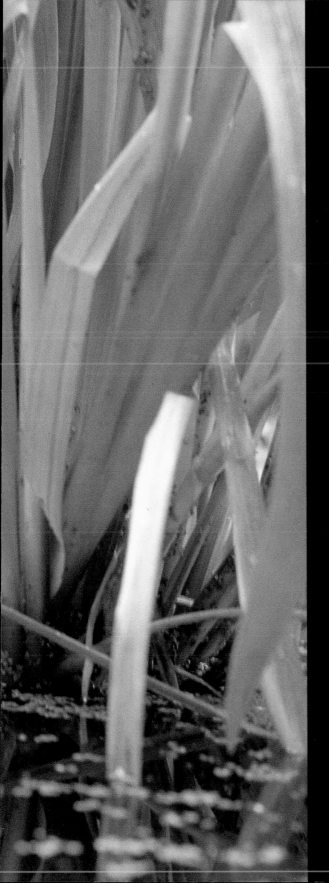

Looking after your pond

Ponds and water features can soon look murky and become infested with weeds if they are not looked after. In this chapter, discover how to keep water clear and algae free, while guarding against pests that threaten to destroy your display. There is also advice on caring for your pond season by season, comprehensive information on choosing and looking after fish, and tips on how to make your water feature or pond safe.

Keeping water clear

Algae are minute plants that grow rapidly in sunlight, quickly turning a crystal clear pond murky green or brown, especially in hot weather. Keeping pond water clear is a major challenge and you may need to use a combination of controls to reduce algal growth.

Floating barley straw

Inexpensive and environmentally friendly, barley straw removes nitrogen from the water, thereby starving algae. The best course of action is to introduce one or two mesh bags or pads of straw into your pond in early spring. You can either float the bags or pads, or submerge them just beneath the surface of the water, if possible near to a fountain or waterfall because oxygen speeds up the decomposition of the straw. Replace the straw when it has turned black.

Investing in pond filters

There are two main types of pond filtration: mechanical and biological. Mechanical filtration captures solid particles from the water in a filter that needs to be removed for cleaning every so often. Biological filtration uses beneficial bacteria to break down organic matter. It can take time to become effective while the active bacteria develop in your system and the filter must be cleaned at intervals as it becomes blocked. For a more permanent solution to algal growth, a biological filter is best used in conjunction with an ultra-violet clarifier.

Using proprietary products

There are many proprietary products available that can give instant results. To use them successfully, however, it is important to follow the manufacturer's instructions carefully and to know the exact volume of water you are treating. Many of these products use copper-based chemicals, which remove oxygen from the water and so harm fish. Excessive doses may also kill some plants. Another disadvantage of using these products is that the dead algae remain in the pond where their decay increases the toxicity of the water.

Adding oxygenating plants

The main function of oxygenating plants is to purify and clear the water by using up nutrients and occluding light, so preventing the growth of algae. During daylight hours in the growing season, they also contribute a certain amount of oxygen to the water. However, these submerged perennial plants mostly die back in the winter, and like all other plants they give off carbon dioxide at night, so they need to be kept under control. When pulling out excess oxygenating plants, bear in mind that they provide habitat for wildlife: not only do they harbour insect larvae but newts and fish lay their eggs among the leaves. For this reason, leave the prunings on a sheet of plastic close to the water for a day to enable wildlife to return to the pond.

Examples of oxygenators

- *Callitriche*
- *Ceratophyllum demersum*
- *Hygrophylla polysperma*
- *Myriophyllum verticillatum*
- *Potamogeton crispus*
- *Potamogeton densus*
- *Ranunculus aquatilis*
- *Utricularia vulgaris*

Covering the water surface

Keeping light out of the water prevents algae from thriving, so plants that cover the surface are very useful. Shading the surface also helps to regulate the water temperature. Don't cover the whole pond or you'll miss the reflections on the water's surface and be unable to enjoy pet fish. Aim to cover about a third of the surface. Water lilies (*below*) are commonly used for this; water hawthorn (*Aponogeton distachyos*), brandy bottles (*Nuphar*), and water fringe (*Nymphoides peltata*) are also good choices.

Encouraging frogs and toads

In early spring, when frogs and toads emerge from hibernation and lay their eggs in your pond, they should be welcomed. Tadpoles are particularly beneficial in a pond because they help to keep it free of algae and organic pond debris, but make sure that you remove any dead tadpoles from the water using a fine-mesh net. Unfortunately, all this wildlife activity may disturb plants, so it's a good idea to check that they are firmly installed in their baskets from time to time.

Sterilizing new plants

To help prevent algae forming, as well as reducing the spread of fish and plant diseases, wash new plants in a weak salt solution and then in fresh water before introducing them to the pond. Alternatively, you can use a mild sterilizing solution – there are several proprietary brands available. For decorative features that contain no plants or fish, you can add sterilizing tablets or solution to keep the water clear. Follow the manufacturer's instructions, and never use sterilants in planted ponds.

Aiming for a natural balance

The ideal solution for algae control is the creation of a natural balance that won't allow it to develop freely. If green water persists, reduce the light getting into the water and lower nutrient levels by removing dead foliage regularly and planting greedy plants, such as water lilies, and oxgenators to use up nutrients. Changing the water only introduces fresh nutrients, but is unavoidable in small ponds prone to evaporation. Here, you may need proprietary products to keep water clear.

Dealing with pond weeds

A pond is really just a flowerbed but with more water in it than soil and, like a flowerbed, it is just as easily infected with unwanted weeds.

Controlling duckweed The most common floating weed is duckweed. It is normally introduced to ornamental ponds by weed-infested newly bought plants or transported on birds' feet. The best way to remove it is with a small hand net, then leave the weeds to dry beside the pond before adding them to the compost heap. Goldfish and carp will eat a certain amount of duckweed, too.

Home for wildlife Although duckweed is a problem plant, it does provide a home for a multitude of wildlife – insect larvae, tadpoles, and baby newts, in particular, thrive when hidden in the dense mat. If you empty your net of duckweed onto a pebble beach or plastic sheet placed next to the water and allow the weed to dry for a day or so, you will find that the wildlife it is holding will return to the pond. You can also catch a number of pests in this way, such as the Greater Water Beetle, and also excess snails. These are easily spotted, and it is worthwhile removing and disposing of them.

Removing problem plants New ponds that are full of nutrients and receive plenty of sunlight are readily infected with blanket weed. The spores are blown in on the wind, but they are also present, although invisible, on most of the plants you buy. Much of it can be scooped out with a net or wound around a stout cane or garden rake. Repeated removal will usually bring it under control until the natural ageing of the pond eliminates it. There are several proprietary products that can help to control blanketweed, but they must be used repeatedly. Using straw to control pond algae has proved very successful in most situations. All types of straw seem to work, but barley straw is most effective. From early spring to late autumn, use up to 50g of straw per square metre of water surface. After about six months, the straw will decay and turn black, and should then be removed.

Keeping ornamentals in check Many of the water plants available are, in fact, wild plants that are accustomed to the rough and tumble of the natural world. When protected and tended in your pool, they often exploit this comparative freedom to the full, and the only way to control them is to grow them in baskets. Particular offenders are aquatic grasses and some irises. Keep an eye on them and be ready to cut out excessive growth at any time during the growing season. Water lily varieties too big for your pond can be kept in check by pruning them in spring.

It is a good idea to remove all seedheads just before they ripen. Most aquatic plants produce very large quantities of seed, and if it is allowed to scatter naturally, the plants will rapidly colonize neighbouring baskets and flowerbeds. This natural process will also lead to more delicate, less robust plants being smothered.

The best way to avoid these problems is not to grow any wild plants in the first place, unless you have a special reason. Researching plants at the outset will help you to choose those that are most suitable for your particular pond.

Space invaders Some imported plants are enthusiastic colonizers, making them very damaging to our natural environment, and are best avoided. Invasive plants, such as parrot's feather and curly pondweed, are easy to remove on a garden scale, and should be composted and never released into natural ponds, ditches, or streams. The following plants are particularly invasive:

- *Azolla carolininiana*
- *Crassula helmsleyanum* (New Zealand pygmy weed)
- *Elodea canadensis* (Canadian pondweed)
- *Hydrocotyle ranunculoides* (floating pennywort)
- *Iris pseudacorus* (flag iris)
- *Juncus effusus*
- *Lagarosiphon major* (curly pondweed)
- *Lythrum salicaria*
- *Myriophyllum proserpinacoides*

Myriophyllum aquaticum (parrot's feather)

Lagarosiphon major (curly pondweed)

Hydrocotyle ranunculoides (floating pennywort)

Pond pests

All ponds attract a wide variety of wildlife and, inevitably, some will be potentially damaging to plants, which makes them a nuisance to water gardeners. Fortunately, relatively few pests prey on aquatics and marginals, and these rarely cause serious problems and are easy to control.

Taking preventative measures There are several steps you can take to keep your pond pest-free. Sprays and insecticides are not recommended because they are lethal to wildlife and pond inhabitants. Healthy, well-cared-for plants are better able to resist problems, so if you see a sickly-looking plant, remove it, wash its roots, and replant it in fresh, clean soil. Remove all dead foliage to stop the spread of fungal growths, and inspect plants regularly, cutting out obviously diseased leaves and stems. Bear in mind that some plants, such as pickerel weed (*Pontederia*), develop later in the season – so take care not to uproot plants just because they don't grow as early or as quickly as expected. To guard against pests or diseases being inadvertently introduced to your pond, wash new plants in a mild sterilizing solution or put them in a weak salt solution and rinse them in fresh water before planting them out.

Encouraging predators Frogs, toads, and newts feed on many different insects, slugs, and worms. Make sure that there is plenty of vegetation within easy reach of your pond so that they are tempted to stay nearby out of the breeding season. Provide damp hiding places for them with a few well-placed stones and old logs. You may wish to add fish to your pond, since they also consume a lot of harmful insects, including mosquito and gnat larvae.

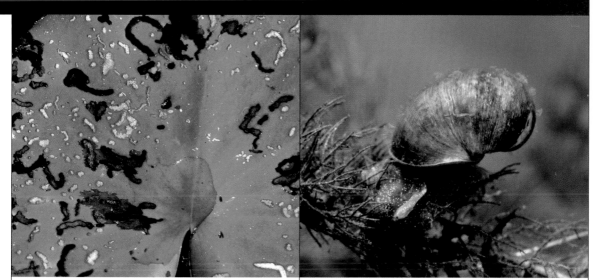

Water lily pests There are two main water lily pests. The water lily beetle emerges in late spring to lay its eggs on lily pads. These hatch into black larvae, which eat the leaves (*above*). Cut away badly damaged pads, and hose off beetles and larvae into the water. The other pests are china mark moth caterpillars, which carve out pieces of leaf, stick them on the undersides of leaves, and live in this "sandwich". Remove the caterpillars by hand.

Underwater assailants Most water snails are harmless and do a good job eating decaying underwater foliage, turning it into useful plant food. The small round snail (*above*) and the Ramshorn snail are the types to have in your pond. The giant pond snail, however, which has a long pointed shell, can be dangerous to plants. Place lettuce leaves on the surface of the water to attract these snails, so that you can remove them with a net.

Aphids and slugs Aphids can weaken water lilies and some marginal and bog plants. Spray the insects with a strong jet of water from a hose and wash them into the water to be eaten by any fish. It may be possible to spray bog garden plants with insecticide, but avoid contaminating the water. Slugs devour plants at the water's edge, such as hostas (*above*). Control them with slug pellets, beer traps, gritty mulches, or copper rings.

Seasonal pond care

A well-planned pond needs the same kind of maintenance as an ordinary flowerbed, but it will need cleaning out well after four or five years.

Winter

At this time of year there is little to do, unless you have ornamental fish in your pond. The most important thing is to ensure fresh air reaches the water if ice forms on the surface. Ice traps poisonous gases, such as methane, which form naturally as vegetation rots down. Keep a hole free from ice so that the gases can disperse. Electrical heaters are available for this, or you can simply float an old tennis ball on the pond. If the ball gets stuck in the ice, free it with hot water. The ball will also help to prevent rigid ponds from cracking as the icy surface expands, since it absorbs some of the pressure. On no account break the ice with a hammer – it will concuss and kill the fish.

Do not feed your fish at this time of year, even if it is icy. Their digestive systems do not work at low temperatures, and they will be hibernating or very lethargic.

Spring

This is the best time to re-assess your planting of both marginals and deep-water aquatics. Some of the former may have grown too big and may need trimming back. Others may need to be lifted and relocated to more satisfactory positions. Gaps can be filled by dividing up your existing stock or buying new plants.

When repotting marginals where the plant is at or just under the water level, don't forget to replace the gravel that keeps the soil in place. Submerged plants will need larger pebbles to prevent the fish from digging them out.

Check that any electrical equipment is clean and in working order, and when frost is no longer a threat, install any pumps that have been taken out for the winter.

Start feeding the fish again, but not more than once every two or three days to start with, increasing the rations as the water gets gradually warmer. Remove any netting to allow free plant growth.

Keep an airhole for fish by floating a tennis ball in icy weather.

Replace the gravel around pond plants to keep soil in place.

Summer

The warm, lazy days of summer are when you can really relax and enjoy your pond. Nevertheless, there is still some maintenance work to be done. Dying and dead foliage should be trimmed away, in particular lily pads that die back naturally throughout the season. Keep an eye out, too, for any signs of disease that might be affecting plants and fish.

In hot weather, especially if you have a fountain or waterfall, the evaporation rate can be quite high. You may even be led to think that the pond has sprung a leak when the water level drops quickly. So keep reservoirs and pools regularly topped up. Hot weather also lowers the oxygen content of the water. If you notice your fish gasping at the pond surface, use a hose or watering can to spray fresh water onto it for a while.

Some plants such as "oxygenators" grow profusely during the summer, but they can be controlled by gently pulling out the surplus. Remove annual and perennial weeds as they occur, mainly among your marginals.

Autumn

This is the time to clear up at the end of the season. Deadhead marginals, which often set large quantities of seed, to prevent them from going on to germinate in unwanted places. Cut back dead foliage and put some netting over the pond to collect as many falling leaves from nearby trees and shrubs as possible. The netting will also protect your fish, when the lack of cover exposes them to the eyes of passing herons.

Reduce the amount of food you give to the fish, and stop feeding them altogether at the first frost. Also, place a 60cm (24in) length of ceramic drain pipe in the bottom of the pond for them to shelter in.

Check over associated structures, such as decking, ornamental bridges, and walls. Repair damage, cracks, subsidence, or splitting, which will only get worse in the winter months ahead.

Remove dying or dead foliage throughout summer.

Net your pond to catch falling autumn leaves.

Dividing pond plants

Many water plants are vigorous and easily increased by division. In spring, just as your plants are starting to grow again, divide those whose root systems have outgrown their baskets.

Tip for success

Flushing old compost and soil away with a garden hose before dividing the plants will make the job easier.

1 Lift the aquatic plants you want to divide out of their positions, and take them out of their baskets. You may need to cut the basket away in order to release well-rooted, older plants.

2 Pull the plant apart into pieces of manageable size. You may need two forks placed back to back to do this. If you need to cut the tangled roots with a knife, do so as carefully as possible to avoid too much damage.

3 Using a sharp knife, slice through sections of main root or rhizome, pulling the bundle apart as you go, and retaining as many new fibrous roots as you can. Don't make the new sections too small.

4 To help the new plants develop, cut back about two-thirds of the original length of the foliage and stems. This will encourage healthy new root growth to make strong plants for the coming season.

5 Place the best pieces in baskets filled with good soil, so that the crowns (where the stems meet the roots) are just above the soil surface. Cover the top of the basket with stones to prevent fish disturbing the soil. Replace in the water.

Adding fish to your pond

Fish give character and movement to a pond and will quickly learn to respond to their owners, especially at feeding time. Buy the fish in late spring when the water is warm.

Pond size requirements

The rule of thumb is "an inch of fish to a square foot of water surface (2.5cm per 30cm of water)". Using this, you can estimate how many fish your pond can accommodate. But remember that they will continue to grow, so allow for this.

As well as providing enough surface area for your fish to breathe properly, your pool also needs an area where it is at least 75–100cm (30in–39in) deep to maintain an ice-free place for them to rest in winter. If you want to keep koi carp, this area needs to be 1.2m (4ft) deep.

Fountains and waterfalls provide extra oxygen, but don't let this tempt you to overstock.

Estimate how many fish your pond will take before stocking up.

Choosing suitable fish

The ordinary goldfish is really the best ornamental fish for a garden pond. Choose fish that are small and compact, and swimming purposefully. Avoid fish that have torn fins, are listless, or have blood stains, small white dots, or fluffy growths on them.

Fantail goldfish are small and compact, but not as hardy as common goldfish.

Goldfish come in many delightful varieties but the more exotic ones are best kept in aquaria rather than ponds. Golden orfe swim mainly on the surface but they really need a pond at least 3m (10ft) long because they can jump out of smaller ponds if startled. Koi and other carp also need larger pools to thrive, and they eat a lot of plants.

Suitable fish for ponds

- Goldfish: Shubunkins, Fantails, Golden comet, Sarasa comet
- Golden orfe
- Mirror carp
- Crucian carp
- Koi carp
- Golden rudd
- Tench

Common goldfish are the best fish for a small garden pond.

Introducing new fish to a pond

Fish are very sensitive to knocks and sudden changes in temperature. It is therefore important to be very gentle when releasing the fish you have bought into their new environment. They are usually supplied in a plastic bag inflated with oxygen, which will last for only a limited time.

Avoid bumping the bag against anything solid. Float it onto the surface of the water to allow the temperature inside the bag to adjust to that of your pond. Open the bag to allow fresh air inside to replace the oxygen. After about 20 minutes, gently tip the fish out of the bag into the pond. The fish will hide away for a couple of days initially, but will soon regain their confidence.

Release the fish when water in the bag has had time to adjust to the pond temperature.

Fish-friendly planting

Your pond is a biological system, and the plants you have in it are very important to the welfare of your fish. Firstly, floating foliage provides shade and cover from predators, like herons. Secondly, all the plants in and around the edges of a pond take up fish waste matter with their roots and so keep the water in good condition, as well as providing extra cover and shade for the fish.

Suitable plants for ponds

- *Acorus calumus*
- *Aponogeton distachyos*
- *Butomus umbellatus*
- *Caltha*
- *Iris*
- *Myosotis scorpioides*
- *Nuphar lutea*
- *Nymphaea*
- *Sagittaria*

Iris laevigata

Nuphar lutea (spatterdock)

Caring for fish

In a well-planted, balanced pond, ornamental fish will more or less look after themselves, but there are steps you can take to keep them healthy and stress-free. Maintaining water quality is important, as is providing food and protection when necessary.

Feeding fish

Since pond fish hibernate during the winter, they need feeding in the warmer months both to satisfy their energy and growth requirements and to build up reserves to see them through their winter sleep. Start feeding in early spring and continue until the autumn frosts. Once the temperatures drop, fish are no longer able to digest food.

Artificial food There is a wide variety of proprietary brands to choose from. Floating pellets and flakes are particularly popular because they bring the fish to the surface where they can be seen more easily. All fish foods should be given only once a day at first, when you start feeding in spring. As the water warms up in summer, the amount can be increased but be careful not to overfeed fish because this can lead to disease. A good basic rule to follow is to give no more food than the fish can eat in three or four minutes.

Live food Your pond will produce some live food, such as gnat and mosquito larvae, but you should supplement this with prepared high-protein foods, such as tubifex worms, white worms (*Enchytraeus*), daphnia, or frozen live food. Feeding a variety of these foods will ensure the best balanced diet. Your fish will obtain additional vitamins and nourishment by grazing on submerged water weed and algae on leaves and underwater stones.

Frozen fish food is usually supplied in strip packs. Each strip contains small food portions.

Protecting fish from predators

The most common and dangerous predator is the heron, which usually appears at around dawn. There is no reliable defence except to cover your pond with a net, mounted high enough so as to not interfere with plant growth. Nets will also protect your fish from cats, but they do have drawbacks, being both unsightly and difficult to erect.

You may prefer to provide alternative protection in the form of water lily pads and other plants that cover the water's surface, under which fish can hide. Even more effective is a length of clay drainpipe or well-weathered concrete pipe placed at the bottom of the pond to act as an air-raid shelter.

Other predators that attack fish are water beetles, dragonfly larvae, and fish lice. Catch beetles and dragonfly larvae whenever you notice them. Bait beetle larvae by tying a small piece of meat to a length of cotton thread and dangling it low in the water. The larvae will bite into the meat and can then be fished out. Fish lice are clearly visible on fish and should be removed. Hold the affected fish in a damp cloth, gently pick off the lice with tweezers, and then destroy them. Disinfect any wounds on the fish with salt solution.

Small garden ponds are particularly attractive to young herons because they often provide easy fishing.

Breeding goldfish

In spring and autumn, the torpedo-shaped male fish can be seen chasing the plumper females. Goldfish start breeding when they are 8–10cm (3–4in) long, laying their eggs in dense clumps of water weed.

Since both eggs and newly hatched fry are eaten by the parents, as well as by insect predators and other fish, few survive. Those that do are either black or olive green. The majority will be olive green, which are reversions to the wild fish and will dominate future breeding, eventually eliminating the golden strain. They are best removed with a net and destroyed; do not release them into natural waters. Keep only dark black fry, some of which may even start to turn gold in their first year.

Goldfish will often produce lots of fry in the first season and then appear not to produce any in subsequent years. This is usually because the pond is fully stocked with fish and so all the eggs and fry are eaten.

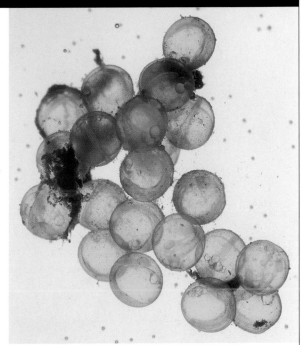

Goldfish eggs are amber-coloured spheres laid by the females and then fertilized by the males.

Common problems

Many people tend to overstock their ponds, particularly if they have fountains and waterfalls which increase the amount of oxygen in the water, thereby supporting greater numbers of fish. Usually, the fish will fare well – until there is a power cut or the weather is particularly hot. Then they start gasping at the surface. If this should happen, spray the pond with a strong jet of water from a hose for several minutes, and reduce the number of fish in the pond.

Diseases are always present in pond water, and weak or injured fish may succumb to them. If caught early, many can be treated. The most common problem is white spot, which appears as little white dots on the body and fins of fish. (It is not to be confused with the white spots on the gills of breeding males.) Proprietary cures are available. Fin rot and ulcers also occur, both of which have specific treatments. If you suspect that your fish are diseased, consult a vet.

Providing shelter from too much sun and a good diet help to keep your fish healthy, active, and disease-free. Always quarantine new fish if you can and avoid injury by removing sharp stones and insect pests from the pond.

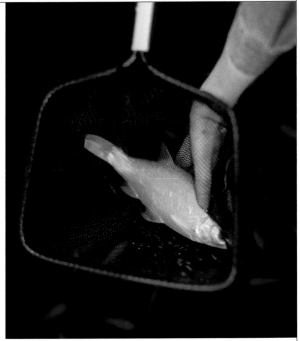

When catching fish be as gentle as possible and steady the fish to prevent injury.

Making your pond safe

Water features make important and beautiful additions to any garden but they can present a number of hazards that you should be aware of. Taking a few simple precautions will help to minimize the dangers.

What are the dangers? Sunken ponds are potentially dangerous, so erect barriers or find other ways of making them safe. Prevent children from falling in a pond by surrounding it with sturdy fencing, for example. Unstable stepping stones or paving are also dangerous, but good building practice should prevent these. Maintain electrical appliances well, and treat wooden surfaces to remove algal growth and to prevent them becoming slippery.

Bring in the experts Ignoring the principles of proper construction can be expensive, not only in terms of potential injury but also as a result of costly, and needless, repairs. If you are in any doubt, call in professional help. It is also illegal to connect electricity supplies yourself, unless you are a qualified electrician. You can plug many pumps into an existing indoor electricity supply, but thread the cable through reinforced piping to protect it (*above*).

Self-contained features and patios Free-standing water features present few safety problems but you will need to ensure that all electrical connections are not only hidden from sight and inaccessible to children, but also impossible for pets to dig up. Surrounding stonework must be firmly installed if it is to be walked on. Follow the same safety guidelines when laying patio paving and any associated lighting.

Protective pond covers If your garden is used by babies and young children, it is best not to have a pond – a small patio fountain without any accessible water is a safer option. However, if you do want a pond, buy a rigid metal grille that fits over the surface. There are many designs available; choose one that is strong enough to support your child's weight and that is secured just above the water. A sheet of netting over the pond is not strong enough to keep children safe.

Plant guide

The aquatic and moisture-loving plants in this guide are grouped according to the depth of water they require, from water lilies that like relatively deep water to bog plants that just require damp soil. Many have the RHS Award of Garden Merit, which means they are excellent plants for the garden.

Key to plant symbols

ᵠ   Plants given the RHS Award of Garden Merit

Preference for sun or shade

☼   Full sun

☼   Partial or dappled shade

☀   Full shade

Hardiness ratings

❄   Plants that need protection from frost over winter

❄❄   Plants that survive outside in mild regions or sheltered sites

❄❄❄   Fully hardy plants

❀   Tender plants that do not tolerate any degree of frost

Pond depth

PD   Refers to the depth of water the plant needs, measured from the top of the soil in the pond basket to the surface

Water lilies (At–Od)

Nymphaea 'Attraction'

This wide-spreading and free-flowering lily is suitable for larger pools. Garnet-red flowers in mid- to late summer are set off by green leaves. Flower colour is best in established plants; if moved they tend to produce white or very pale blooms.

S: 2m (6ft), **PD**: 1–1.2m (3–4ft)
✿✿✿ ☀ ♔

Nymphaea 'Escarboucle'

Named after a talismanic jewel in French literature, this is the best of all red water lilies. It has huge (up to 30cm/12in wide) crimson flowers with a central boss of brilliant orange stamens in mid- to late summer. It performs best when well established.

S: 1.5m (5ft), **PD**: 60–100cm (2–3ft)
✿✿✿ ☀ ♔

Nymphaea 'Froebelii'

This is an excellent variety for tubs and small ponds. It has purple-green leaves and small blood-red flowers that are produced in profusion from midsummer until autumn. It is small enough to allow several plants to be grown together.

S: 75cm (30in), **PD**: 30–45cm (12–18in)
✿✿✿ ☀

Nymphaea 'Gladstoneana'

Huge white waxy blooms the size of large dinner plates float among dark green circular leaves, which have characteristic brown marked stems. Flowering is from late spring to early autumn. A vigorous grower, it suits only large ponds.

S: 3m (10ft), **PD**: 1–2m (3–6ft)
✿✿✿ ☀ ♔

Nymphaea 'Gonnère'

This is a beautiful water lily for medium-sized pools. In mid- to late summer, it has double white globular flowers comprised of pointed petals, held together by green sepals that emphasize their whiteness. Its leaves are bronze-green when young.

S: 1.5m (5ft), **PD**: 60–75cm (24–30in)
✿✿✿ ☀ ♔

Nymphaea 'James Brydon'

The fully double, almost carmine flowers, produced in mid- to late summer, bring to mind a waterborne peony. They float among dark purplish-green leaves that are often flecked with maroon. This is an ideal plant for medium and small ponds.

S: 60cm (24in), **PD**: 45–60cm (18–24in)
✿✿✿ ☀ ♔

Nymphaea 'Laydekeri Lilacea'
Delightful in a small pond or tub, this plant produces a huge number of small, single flowers that open soft rose-pink and darken with age to a bright carmine. It blooms from late spring to early autumn. The glossy leaves may be blotched with brown.

S: 45cm (18in), **PD**: 30–45cm (12–18in)
❀❀ ☼

Nymphaea 'Lemon Chiffon'
This robust water lily has almost double lemon-yellow flowers, which are produced from late spring until early autumn, and heavily mottled foliage. It is a robust plant, suitable for small and medium pools, as well as containers.

S: 75cm (30in), **PD**: 30–60cm (12–24in)
❀❀ ☼

Nymphaea 'Marliacea Albida'
From late spring to early autumn, this outstanding variety has large, fragrant white blooms, flushed with pale pink, that stand just above water level. Its deep green leaves have purple or red undersides. This is a plant for larger pools.

S: 1.2m (4ft), **PD**: 60–100cm (2–3ft)
❀❀❀ ☼ ♈

Nymphaea 'Marliacea Chromatella'
This old favourite dates from 1877. Its soft yellow flowers, which appear in mid- to late summer, have deeper yellow centres and pink-flushed outer sepals. They float among olive-green leaves, which are blotched with bronze marbling.

S: 1.5m (5ft), **PD**: 60–100cm (2–3ft)
❀❀❀ ☼ ♈

Nymphaea odorata var. minor
Ideal for small ponds and tubs, this miniature water lily produces very fragrant, tiny star-shaped white flowers from late spring to early autumn. The blooms are set off by soft green leaves with dark red undersides.

S: 45cm (18in), **PD**: 25–30cm (10–12in)
❀❀ ☼

Nymphaea 'Odorata Sulphurea'
Heavily mottled foliage surrounds canary-yellow, star-shaped flowers in mid- to late summer. The blooms have many thin petals, which give them a distinctive appearance. Despite its name, this variety does not have much scent. It is good for small pools.

S: 75cm (30in), **PD**: 30–60cm (12–24in)
❀❀❀ ☼

Water lilies (Py–Tu)

Nymphaea 'Pygmaea Helvola'
A delightful water lily that produces many star-shaped pale yellow flowers in mid- to late summer – a mature plant may have as many as 30 blooms out at once. Its leaves are heavily mottled with bronze-brown. It is best for small ponds, troughs, and tubs.

S: 45cm (18in), **PD**: 25–30cm (9–12in)
❄❄ ☼ ♈

Nymphaea 'Pygmaea Rubra'
This plant is larger than other Pygmaea varieties. In mid- to late summer, its flowers open a pleasant rose colour and age to a rich garnet-red, while its green leaves have red undersides. It makes a lovely display in small pools, containers, and tubs.

S: 45cm (18in), **PD**: 20–25cm (8–10in)
❄❄ ☼

Nymphaea 'René Gérard'
Particularly suited to growing in small ponds and containers, this free-flowering water lily has plain green leaves and star-shaped rich rose-coloured flowers splashed with crimson. It blooms from late spring until early autumn.

S: 60cm (24in), **PD**: 30–45cm (12–18in)
❄❄❄ ☼

Nymphaea 'Rose Arey'
A medium-sized water lily with many large fragrant star-shaped flowers that open rose-pink and pale with age. Flowering is from late spring to early autumn. The leaves are a very striking red when young, becoming green, tinged with red, later.

S: 1m (3ft), **PD**: 30–45cm (12–18in)
❄❄❄ ☼

Nymphaea tetragona
The smallest water lily of all is ideal for patio containers. Tiny white flowers, which appear from late spring to early summer, are exact replicas of larger varieties. The leaves are only 5cm (2in) long, usually plain green but sometimes mottled.

S: 30cm (12in), **PD**: 15–25cm (6–10in)
❄❄ ☼

Nymphaea 'Tuberosa Richardsonii'
Apple-green leaves and sepals set off the pure white, peony-like semi-double flowers, which are freely produced from late spring to early autumn. This plant, from North America, is an excellent subject for medium- to large-sized ponds.

S: 1.1m (3½ft), **PD**: 45–75cm (18–30in)
❄❄❄ ☼

Deep water aquatics (Ap–Ra)

Aponogeton distachyos

Water hawthorn is an attractive plant from South Africa with strap-shaped leaves and masses of white flowers that have a delicate, hawthorn-like fragrance. The blooms are plentiful in summer; in the northern hemisphere they appear all year round.

S: 60cm (24in), **PD**: 60cm (24in)
❋❋❋ ☼ ◑ ●

Ceratophyllum demersum

Hornwort is an oxygenator with whorls of green foliage around the stem. It occludes light in the water, which helps to keep algae under control, and provides cover for wildlife. It is easily propagated from cuttings.

S: unlimited, **PD**: 1m (3ft)
❋❋ ☼ ◑ ●

Nuphar lutea

Brandy bottle is a rampant grower with large green pads on the surface and lettuce-like leaves underwater. Cup-shaped yellow flowers, carried well above the water, appear from late spring to early autumn. *N. japonica* is better for small pools.

S: unlimited, **PD**: 60cm–1m (24in–3ft)
❋❋❋ ☼ ◑ ●

Nymphoides peltata

The fringed water lily is becoming increasingly rare in the wild. Small, rounded leaves float on the water's surface; fringed yellow flowers stand above them in mid- to late summer. It needs to be confined to a basket and pruned regularly.

S: unlimited, **PD**: 45–75cm (18–30in)
❋❋❋ ☼ ◑

Orontium aquaticum

If golden rod is planted deep enough, its large, glaucous leaves will float on the surface of the water. In late spring, white rods covered in golden-yellow florets are produced. The plant has a massive root system that helps to keep pond water clear.

S: 60cm (24in), **PD**: 30–45cm (12–18in)
❋❋❋ ☼

Ranunculus aquatilis

This plant thrives in both running and still water and is a good oxygenator. Its submerged leaves are thin and thread-like; those on the surface resemble tiny lily pads. Small white flowers appear in summer. Propagate by root cuttings in midsummer.

S: unlimited, **PD**: 25–45cm (10–18in)
❋❋❋ ☼

Marginals (Ac–Ca)

Acorus calamus 'Argenteostriatus'
The crushed leaves of the deciduous sweet rush give off a strong scent – it was once used as a floor covering. This is a decorative variety with white-striped foliage. The flowers are inconspicuous. Non-invasive, it is suitable for ponds or containers.

H: 75cm (30in), **S**: 30cm (24in), **PD**: 20cm (8in) ❋❋❋ ☼ ☀

Acorus gramineus 'Hakuro-nishiki'
This miniature, almost evergreen plant from the Far East has attractive golden green, tufted foliage. It is useful for decorating small water features, such as barrels and bowls. *A. gramineus* var. *pusillus* is also a miniature but with plain green leaves.

H: 8cm (3in), **S**: 15cm (6in) **PD**: At water level ❋❋ ☼ ☀

Acorus gramineus 'Ogon'
A fairly small, almost evergreen plant with gold-striped green leaves that looks good in water features such as barrels and bowls, as well as in small ponds. Propagate it by division in spring. *A. gramineus* 'Variegatus' has cream-striped leaves.

H: 25cm (10in), **S**: 23cm (9in) **PD**: At water level ❋❋ ☼ ☀

Alisma plantago-aquatica
The water plantain is a deciduous British native with tall spikes of tiny, off-white flowers in summer. It spreads by seed, so remove spent flowerheads to keep it under control. Dragonfly larvae favour this plant, leaving their larval cases on its stems.

H: 60cm (24in), **S**: 45cm (18in) **PD**: 30cm (12in) ❋❋❋ ☼ ☀

Butomus umbellatus
The flowering rush is a British native with slender, deciduous, rush-like leaves and umbels of pink flowers in midsummer. It spreads well in an open position. 'Rosenrot' has darker pink flowers; 'Schneeweisschen' has lovely white blooms.

H: 1m (3ft), **S**: unlimited **PD**: 5–15cm (2–6in) ❋❋❋ ☼ ♛

Calla palustris
This small arum produces a rather dull, greenish-white spathe in late spring, followed by bright scarlet berries. The heart-shaped leaves give it a lush appearance. This is an unusual plant because it is fertilized by snails.

H: 25cm (10in), **S**: 45cm (18in) **PD**: 8cm (3in) ❋❋❋ ☼ ☀

Caltha palustris

The late spring-flowering marsh marigold has golden blooms that brighten up the dullest of days. It has round leaves that contrast well with emerging iris leaves and reeds. The plant was once said to be a cure for fits!

H: 60cm (24in), **S**: 45cm (18in)
PD: At water level ❋❋❋ ☼ ☼ ♛

Caltha palustris *var.* alba

This white marsh marigold has leaves edged with teeth-like indentations. It is a grand contrast to its yellow-flowered relative and flowers twice a year, in spring and in early autumn. Propagate by division in early spring.

H: 45cm (18in), **S**: 30cm (12in)
PD: At water level ❋❋❋ ☼ ☼

Caltha palustris '*Marilyn*'

This cultivar is a great improvement on *C. palustris*. It is more erect, and produces a great number of beautiful rich egg-yolk-yellow flowers. It is best propagated by dividing an older plant in spring, since it won't come true from seed.

H: 60cm (24in); **S**: 30cm (12in)
PD: At water level ❋❋❋ ☼ ☼

Caltha palustris *var.* palustris

This variety produces its yellow flowers in early spring. Plantlets emerge from nodes on the flowering stem, which flop over to bring them into contact with the soil. As a result, this plant can overwhelm its neighbours if not controlled.

H: 1m (3ft), **S**: 75cm (30in)
PD: At water level ❋❋❋ ☼ ☼

Caltha palustris '*Plena*'

A double form with dark chrome-yellow flowers in spring. It is easily increased by division. The Victorians liked to use it as edging for their herbaceous borders.

H: 30cm (12in), **S**: 45cm (18in)
PD: At water level ❋❋ ☼ ☼ ♛

Cardamine pratensis

Lady's smock is one of Britain's prettiest spring-flowering wild plants. The flowers are pinkish-mauve and the leaves were once used in salads. *Cardamine* is propagated by dividing three-year-old plants.

H: 25cm (10in), **S**: 10cm (4in)
PD: At water level ❋❋ ☼ ☼

Marginals (Ca–Ir)

Carex riparia 'Variegata'

Variegated pond sedge is a beautiful deciduous grass with thin green stripes on its almost-white leaves, and brown-black flowerheads in late spring and early summer. It is very invasive and needs to be kept under control in a pond basket.

H: 60–100cm (2–3ft); **S**: unlimited
PD: 8cm (3in) ❄❄❄ ☀ ☀

Cotula coronopifolia

Brass buttons is an Australian annual that colonizes shallow water at the pond's edge. Masses of small yellow flowers emerge from creeping stems in early summer. It is useful for underplanting larger plants grown either as marginals or in containers.

H: 25cm (10in), **S**: 23cm (9in)
PD: At water level ❄❄ ☀

Equisetum arvense

Horsetail is an attractive, if invasive, plant with pinkish-green stems in early spring and feathery green foliage. Make sure that it is well contained so it does not invade stonework at pond edges. The plant is poisonous to animals.

H: 10–30cm (4–12in), **S**: unlimited
PD: At water level ❄❄ ☀ ☀

Equisetum hyemale

This primeval-looking evergreen native plant was once in demand as a pot scourer. It has decorative stems and, since it needs to be kept under control, is excellent for growing in containers. 'Bandit' has yellow banded stems.

H: 75cm (30in), **S**: 30cm (12in)
PD: 10cm (4in) ❄❄❄ ☀

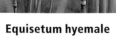

Eriophorum angustifolium

The deciduous cotton grass has thin leaves and soft white flowers like cotton wool in summer. It thrives in very acid soil, and is invasive, so needs to be confined in a basket or container. Even so, it will often disappear, so keep some seed in reserve.

H: 45cm (18in), **S**: unlimited
PD: 5cm (2in) ❄❄❄ ☀ ☀

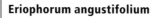

Glyceria maxima *var.* variegata

An attractive tall deciduous grass with cream and green striped leaves, which are tinted purple when they emerge in spring. It is very invasive and should be confined to a container or basket and pruned to prevent it taking over an entire pond.

H: 1m (3ft), **S**: unlimited
PD: At water level ❄❄❄ ☀ ☀

Iris laevigata

The Japanese water iris, with its large mid-blue flowers, is said to be the best blue iris of all. It thrives in a good loam, quickly building up substantial clumps and within three to four years giving a wonderful early summer display.

H: 75cm (30in), **S**: 1m (3ft)
PD: 10–15cm (4–6in) ✳✳✳ ☼ ♛

Iris laevigata 'Liam Johns'

Selected at Rowden Gardens in Devon and named after a family member, this plant has distinctive single grey-white flowers with a violet-blue centre in early summer. The delicate flower colour contrasts well with stronger coloured blooms.

H: 75cm (30in), **S**: 1m (3ft)
PD: 10–15cm (4–6in) ✳✳✳ ☼

Iris laevigata 'Richard Greaney'

This strong-growing variety produces single flowers in early summer that are a remarkably clear and true pale blue. Selected at Rowden Gardens and named after a family member, it enhances the colours of other forms but also stands out alone.

H: 75cm (30in), **S**: 1m (3ft)
PD: 10–15cm (4–6in) ✳✳✳ ☼

Iris laevigata 'Variegata'

The striking, silver-white variegated foliage of this iris is retained throughout the growing season. A vigorous plant, it has blue flowers in summer. It brightens up dull corners and contrasts well with plants that have plain green foliage.

H: 75cm (30in), **S**: 1m (3ft)
PD: 10–15cm (4–6in) ✳✳✳ ☼ ♛

Iris laevigata 'Weymouth Midnight'

The large, double flowers of this variety, produced in early summer, are a magnificent dark blue, with a brilliant white stripe down the middle of each petal. The plant is an asset to any water feature.

H: 75cm (30in), **S**: 1m (3ft)
PD: 10–15cm (4–6in) ✳✳✳ ☼

Iris pseudacorus

The yellow flag is a magnificently boisterous and prolific British wild flower, with yellow flowers with brown markings in early summer. It was adopted as France's *fleur de lys* emblem after a French king hid in a clump to escape his enemies.

H: 1.2m (4ft), **S**: 1m (3ft)
PD: 10–15cm (4–6in) ✳✳✳ ☼ ☽ ♛

Marginals (Ir–Ly)

Iris pseudacorus 'Alba'
This iris is a rather rare plant. It has broad green leaves and pale ivory-white flowers, with a faintly pencilled grey stripe on the tops of the petals. It grows best in a good loam and flowers from late spring to early summer.

H: 1m (3ft), **S**: 60cm (24in)
PD: 15cm (6in) ✻✻ ☼

Iris pseudacorus var. bastardii
Often sold as 'Sulphur Queen', this variety of iris has pale primrose-yellow flowers from late spring to early summer. It is suitable for growing in medium- to large-sized ponds and likes a loamy soil. Propagate by division after flowering.

H: 1m (3ft), **S**: 75cm (30in)
PD: 15cm (6in) ✻✻✻ ☼

Iris pseudacorus 'Flore-Pleno'
This double form is perhaps more curious than beautiful. The late spring to early summer flowers resemble a dishcloth with their layers of sulphur-yellow petals, but it looks striking when grown on its own as a specimen. It thrives in good loam.

H: 1m (3ft), **S**: 75cm (30in)
PD: 15cm (6in) ✻✻✻ ☼

Iris pseudacorus 'Variegata'
The foliage of this iris emerges as primrose-yellow in the spring, becoming overlaid with green as the season advances. By late summer, the leaves are entirely green. The flowers are the same yellow as those of *I. pseudacorus*.

H: 1m (3ft), **S**: 75cm (30in)
PD: 15cm (6in) ✻✻✻ ☼ ♀

Iris versicolor
The American blue flag produces blue-purple flowers in early summer. These are smaller than those of other water irises but compensate by being produced in profusion. The plant is suitable for smaller water features. Grow in a good loam.

H: 75cm (30in), **S**: 75cm (30in)
PD: 5cm (2in) ✻✻✻ ☼ ♀

Iris versicolor 'Kermesina'
This sumptuous form bears magenta-red flowers with white markings in early summer. As with other varieties, propagate by division after flowering. It makes a good partner for the American blue flag, and is suitable for growing in a container.

H: 75cm (30in), **S**: 60cm (24in)
PD: 5cm (2in) ✻✻✻ ☼

Iris versicolor 'Whodunit'
The flowers of this American variety have broad white petals that are heavily overlaid with blue veining, and appear from late spring to early summer. It is a very beautiful form that warrants growing as a specimen plant, and prefers humus-rich soil.

H: 75cm (30in), **S**: 60cm (24in)
PD: 5cm (2in) ❁❁❁ ☼

Juncus effusus f. spiralis
Corkscrew rush has curled, contorted stem-like, tubular leaves – it makes a useful specimen plant where an unusual effect is required. It produces small brown flowers in summer and seeds profusely, so keep it in check with regular deadheading.

H: 30cm (12in), **S**: 45cm (18in)
PD: 5cm (2in) ❁❁❁ ☼

Juncus ensifolius
This is a low-growing, ground-cover plant with grass-like leaves and attractive black flowerheads. However, it is extremely vigorous and needs to be confined to a basket or it will overwhelm other plants. Grow in very shallow water.

H: 23cm (9in), **S**: unlimited
PD: At water level ❁❁❁ ☼ ◐

Lobelia cardinalis
A stately, upright plant with brilliant red flowers from late summer to autumn. There are forms with brown-purple foliage, and white, pink, purple, and scarlet flowers. A short-lived tender plant, it must be brought inside in winter; it can be divided in spring.

H: 1m (3ft), **S**: 25cm (10in)
PD: At water level ❁ ☼ ♈

Lysichiton americanus
The North American yellow skunk cabbage produces striking yellow spathes in early spring, followed by huge leaves. It has a large root system that uses up nutrients in the water, helping to keep it clear of algae. The plant has a musky smell.

H: 75cm (18in), **S**: 1.2m (4ft)
PD: 30cm (12in) ❁❁❁ ☼ ◑ ◐ ♈

Lysichiton camtschatcensis
The white skunk cabbage from China has glistening white spathes in spring. It is a little smaller than its American cousin but does the same job in a pond. In an enclosed space, the flowers can smell unpleasant, but they do look splendid together.

H: 60cm (24in), **S**: 1m (3ft)
PD: 30cm (12in) ❁❁ ☼ ◑ ◐ ♈

Marginals (Me–Sa)

Mentha aquatica
Water mint has highly aromatic red stems and dense clusters of attractive small mauve flowers that appear in summer. Its invasive habit makes it suitable for wilder plantings, but it needs to be confined to a basket.

H: 1m (3ft), **S**: unlimited
PD: At water level ❄❄❄ ☼

Menyanthes trifoliata
The bog bean gets its name from the shape of its leaves. Its intriguing pink- and white-fringed flowers open in spring, and its long prostrate stems often need cutting back. Propagate by division or cuttings.

H: 30cm (12in), **S**: unlimited
PD: 15cm (6in) ❄❄❄ ☼ ☼

Mimulus cardinalis
This North American plant, also known as red monkey musk, produces many small flowers in mid- to late summer whose vivid scarlet colour more than compensates for their size. Cut back after flowering to encourage new growth.

H: 75cm (30in), **S**: 45cm (18in)
PD: At water level ❄ ☼ ♈

Mimulus guttatus
Monkey flower is a North American native that in summer bears masses of yellow blooms, each with several small scarlet spots at the top of the throat. It can overcome smaller plants. Propagate by division or from seed in spring.

H: 75cm (30in); **S**: 30cm (12in)
PD: At water level ❄❄ ☼

Myosotis scorpioides
Water forget-me-not is a charming plant with small, bright blue flowers from late spring to early summer. It seeds enthusiastically but is easy to control. 'Mermaid' is an improved form with larger flowers, and there are white and pink varieties, too.

H: 45cm (18in), **S**: unlimited
PD: At water level ❄❄❄ ☼ ☼

Oenanthe javanica 'Flamingo'
This spreading perennial is grown for its attractive green, white, and purple variegated foliage. Small clusters of tiny white flowers, which appear in late summer, are insignificant. Its roots hang in the water, protecting fish eggs.

H: 30cm (12in), **S**: unlimited
PD: At water level ❄❄ ☼ ☼

Persicaria amphibia

This versatile plant grows in shallow to deep water. The deeper it is, the more the leaves float on the surface, enhancing the pinkish-white flower spikes in summer. It soon degenerates in foul water, so is a good indicator of water conditions.

H: 30cm (12in), **S**: unlimited
PD: 15cm–1m (6in–3ft) ✳✳✳ ☼ ☀

Phragmites australis 'Variegatus'

A magnificent grass with deciduous green leaves decorated with old gold-coloured stripes that set off its purple flowers to perfection in autumn. Since it is a very invasive plant, in a small garden it is suitable only for growing in a container.

H: 2.5m (8ft); **S**: unlimited
PD: 30–100cm (1–3ft) ✳✳✳ ☼

Pontederia cordata

This easy-to-control perennial from North America, commonly known as pickerel weed, has distinctive, glistening, spear-shaped leaves topped by blue flower spikes in late summer. There are white ('Alba') and mauve ('Pink Pons') coloured varieties.

H: 60cm (2ft), **S**: unlimited
PD: 30cm (12in) ✳✳✳ ☼ ♈

Ranunculus flammula

This small buttercup has plentiful little yellow flowers in summer and is useful as an underplanter, such as in baskets of iris. It has a rather scruffy habit. The subspecies *minimus* forms compact cushions 20cm (8in) wide, covered in golden flowers.

H: 30cm (12in), **S**: 60cm (24in)
PD: At water level ✳✳✳ ☼

Ranunculus lingua 'Grandiflorus'

Greater spearwort is a tall, graceful perennial that produces in summer golden yellow buttercup-like flowers carried on reddish-green stems among lance-shaped leaves. It is an enthusiastic wanderer, so is best confined to a basket.

H: 1m (3ft), **S**: unlimited
PD: 30cm (12in) ✳✳✳ ☼

Sagittaria sagittifolia

This is an excellent marginal with attractive, arrow-shaped foliage. Spikes of white flowers appear in late summer. It grows from a round tuber favoured by ducks, hence its other name of duck potato. Confine to a basket in smaller ponds.

H: 60cm (24in), **S**: unlimited
PD: At water level ✳✳✳ ☼

Marginals (Sa–Za)

Saururus cernuus
The North American swamp lily looks nothing like a lily – in fact, the spikes of creamy-white flowers look more like pipe cleaners when, in late summer, they hang over the heart-shaped leaves. It is vigorous and needs to be confined in small ponds.

H: 60cm (24in), **S**: unlimited
PD: 30cm (12in) ✽✽ ☼

Schoenoplectus lacustris *subsp.* tabernaemontani '*Albescens*'
A tall, graceful rush with glaucous stems, decorated with cream stripes, that brightens up any planting. Its height makes it prone to being blown over when planted in a basket. Increase by division in spring.

H: 2m (6ft), **S**: 60cm (24in)
PD: 25cm (10in) ✽✽ ☼

Schoenoplectus lacustris *subsp.* tabernaemontani '*Zebrinus*'
Similar to 'Albescens' but shorter, zebra rush has bold yellow bands all the way up the stem. Grow it on its own in a container or surround it with unvariegated plants in small ponds and water features.

H: 1.2m (4ft), **S**: 45cm (18in)
PD: 25cm (10in) ✽✽ ☼

Scrophularia auriculata '*Variegata*'
Water figwort is a useful tall herbaceous perennial with striking cream-edged foliage. The flowers are unremarkable but attract bees. Grow in a sheltered spot and propagate by cuttings in summer.

H: 1m (3ft); **S**: 60cm (24in)
PD: 8cm (3in) ✽✽ ☼ ☼

Sparganium erectum
Grassy, deciduous or semi-evergreen foliage gives rise to attractive mace-shaped seedheads in autumn. This plant is very invasive, so confine it to a basket in small ponds. Where grown close to lakesides, ducks feed greedily on the seedheads.

H: 1m (3ft), **S**: unlimited
PD: 30cm (12in) ✽✽✽ ☼ ☼

Typha angustifolia
The lesser reed mace is an elegant but invasive plant with brown seedheads that are popular with flower arrangers (who fix them with hairspray to prevent them exploding). It is a tall plant that needs weighting down when grown in a basket.

H: 2m (6ft), **S**: unlimited
PD: 60cm (24in) ✽✽✽ ☼

Typha latifolia

The great reed mace (often wrongly called bulrush) is a larger and more invasive version of *T. angustifolia*. In small gardens, grow it in a patio container for its seedheads. When the "maces" burst, they produce a fine down, once used for stuffing pillows.

H: 3m (10ft), **S**: unlimited
PD: 60cm (24in) ❄❄❄ ☼

Typha latifolia '*Variegata*'

This variety is slightly less invasive but even so is best grown in a large container, such as a plastic laundry basket, which keeps the runners together and produces a massed effect. Otherwise, new plants are too widely spaced to look good.

H: 1.2m (4ft); **S**: unlimited
PD: 60cm (24in) ❄❄ ☼

Typha minima

This intriguing miniature has thin, grassy leaves and tiny round blackish-brown "maces" about the size of a pea. Mixed with small water lilies and other dwarf marginals, it is ideal for miniature water features. It is found in Europe and northern Asia.

H: 60cm (24in), **S**: unlimited
PD: 30cm (12in) ❄❄❄ ☼

Veronica beccabunga

Brooklime is an excellent almost evergreen spreading plant that can be used to underplant more robust companions. It produces clusters of tiny bright blue flowers with white centres. It has fleshy stems and oval, shiny leaves. Confine it to a basket.

H: 30cm (12in), **S**: unlimited
PD: 8cm (3in) ❄❄❄ ☼

Zantedeschia aethiopica '*Crowborough*'

The arum lily has lush, pointed, dark green leaves and beautiful white, scented flowers from late spring to midsummer. 'Crowborough' is the hardiest variety, but the root must not be allowed to freeze in winter.

H: 1.2m (4ft), **S**: 75cm (30in)
PD: 15cm (6in) ❄❄ ☼ ◐

Zantedeschia aethiopica '*Green Goddess*'

Larger than 'Crowborough', this variety has stunning green flowers from late spring to midsummer. The blooms develop white centres as they age, distinguishing them from the leaves. Keep the root frost-free.

H: 1.5m (5ft), **S**: 1m (3ft)
PD: 15cm (6in) ❄❄ ☼ ◐ ●

Bog plants (Ac–Ca)

Aconitum napellus
In early summer, this perennial's curiously hooded blue-violet flowers make an interesting contribution to damper parts of the garden. It is very poisonous, however. Thin out the tuberous roots every four years or so to encourage flowering.

H: 1m (3ft), **S**: 45cm (18in)
❄❄❄ ☼ ◐

Actaea matsumurae '*White Pearl*'
A very attractive and useful perennial that produces graceful plumes of white flowers in autumn, followed by brown seedheads. The dark green foliage is handsomely divided. Increase by division when the plant re-emerges in spring.

H: 1.2m (4ft), **S**: 75cm (30in)
❄❄❄ ☼ ◐ ◑

Actaea simplex '*Atropurpurea*'
Dark brown-bronze leaves are set off by spikes of purple- or pink-flushed white flowers in autumn. Good forms are 'Brunette' and 'James Compton'. Their late flowering is particularly useful when most flowers are dying back for winter.

H: 1.2m (4ft), **S**: 60cm (24in)
❄❄❄ ☼

Ajuga reptans '*Multicolor*'
Bugle is a particularly good plant for brightening up a dull corner. It has brownish-bronze foliage enlivened with yellow, pink, and green, and blue flowers in spring. It is an excellent evergreen ground-cover plant that tolerates shade.

H: 15cm (6in); **S**: unlimited
❄❄❄ ☼ ◐

Anagallis tenella
A delightful and very pretty evergreen perennial that creeps over the soil at the water's edge to form a dense carpet of tiny leaves decorated with rose-pink flowers. Also known as bog pimpernel, it is a useful plant for small water features. Propagate by division.

H: 2.5cm (1in); **S**: unlimited
❄❄ ☼ ◐

Aruncus aethusifolius
It is difficult to believe that tiny goat's beard is related to its larger cousins – it makes a compact clump of ferny foliage, topped by small spikes of tiny white flowers in early summer. Grow in troughs and containers alongside other moisture-loving plants.

H: 30cm (12in), **S**: 20cm (8in)
❄❄❄ ☼ ◐ ♈

Aruncus dioicus

A large, robust perennial with handsome fern-like foliage and astilbe-like plumes of creamy-white flowers in summer. The male form has the prettiest flowers and does not scatter seedlings everywhere. It thrives in both dry and damp situations.

H: 1.5m (5ft), **S**: 1.2m (4ft)
❄❄❄ ☼ ◐ ♛

Aruncus dioicus '*Kneiffii*'

This small variety has beautiful, very finely cut, thread-like foliage. It was introduced in 1889 and is ideal for smaller gardens and containers. Team it with smaller ferns, damp-loving irises, and small plants with simple foliage shapes.

H: 75cm (30in), **S**: 45cm (18in)
❄❄ ☼ ◐

Astilbe x arendsii

The best-known group of astilbes, which are clump-forming perennials, vary in size and flowering period, and come in a range of colours, including red, purple, white, pink, and lavender. Foliage colour also varies. Look out for 'White Gloria', 'Ceres', and 'Fanal'.

H: 60cm–1m (2–3ft), **S**: 60cm (24in)
❄❄❄ ☼ ◐

Astilbe chinensis *var.* pumila

A small but vigrous perennial with lavender-pink flower spikes in late summer. It likes damper conditions than most astilbes and makes a good partner for small irises such as *I. chrysographes*, whose leaves contrast well with astilbe's fern-like foliage.

H: 45cm (18in), **S**: 30cm (12in)
❄❄❄ ☼ ◐ ♛

Astilbe chinensis taquetii '*Superba*'

A superb plant for large bog gardens. Its silver-magenta flowers bring welcome colour to the garden in late summer and early autumn. Plant alongside earlier-flowering actaeas and propagate by division in spring.

H: 1.2m (4ft), **S**: 1m (3ft)
❄❄❄ ☼ ◐ ♛

Carex elata '*Aurea*'

Found in the Norfolk Broads by E.A. Bowles (after whom several grasses are named), this deciduous damp-loving perennial has brilliant golden-yellow foliage. Creamy flowers appear in spring, which develop into brown spikes.

H: 60cm (24in), **S**: 45cm (18in)
❄❄❄ ☼ ♛

Bog plants (Ca–Ge)

Carex pendula
Weeping sedge is a graceful but substantial grass, with flowering stems arching attractively over broad green leaves. It mixes well with ferns and hostas. Keep in check, however, as it will seed freely. 'Moonraker' is a good variegated form.

H: 1.2m (4ft), **S**: 1m (3ft)
❋❋❋ ☼ ◑

Darmera peltata
This slow-spreading perennial seems too large to be related to the tiny saxifrages usually grown in troughs. In spring, tall stems carry masses of pink flowers. The fading flowers are replaced by leaves that look like large soup plates. It can be rather invasive.

H: 1.2m (4ft), **S**: unlimited
❋❋❋ ☼ ◑ ☀ ♆

Dierama pulcherrimum
Angel's fishing rod is an evergreen perennial from South Africa. It is a sight to behold in midsummer when long, arching stems appear from grass-like foliage, carrying pendulous flowers in many hues, including white, pink, magenta, and lavender.

H: 1.5m (5ft), **S**: 30cm (12in)
❋❋ ☼

Eupatorium cannabinum 'Flore-Pleno'
With substantial heads of rose-pink double flowers in midsummer, hemp agrimony makes an impression in any bog garden. Propagate by division in early spring. It prefers chalky soil, and makes a smaller plant in acid soil.

H: 1.2m (4ft) 1m (3ft)
❋❋❋ ☼ ◑

Eupatorium purpureum
This imposing perennial with tall, purple-flecked stems carries whorls of pointed leaves and large purple-pink flowerheads in autumn. It is a good choice for larger bog gardens. Propagate from cuttings in late spring and protect it from slugs.

H: 2m (6ft), **S**: 1m (3ft)
❋❋❋ ☼ ◑

Eupatorium rugosum 'Chocolate'
With its stiff brown stems and toothed, nettle-like leaves in a wonderful shade of dull purple, this plant adds colour all season. In early autumn, its white flowers stand out well against the foliage. Propagate by division in spring.

H: 1.2m (4ft), **S**: 60cm (24in)
❋❋ ☼ ◑ ♆

Euphorbia palustris
Marsh spurge makes a substantial clump that is covered in late spring with acid-yellow flowers. It is a splendid bog plant that can be propagated by division when it first comes into growth. It produces poisonous milky juice when cut.

H: 1.2m (4ft); **S**: 1m (3ft)
❄❄ ☼ ☼

Filipendula purpurea
Sprays of magenta-pink flowers in summer and large palmate green leaves make this clump-forming perennial a real eyecatcher. Introduced from Japan in 1823, it has long been a favourite for bog gardens. Propagate by division in spring.

H: 1.2m (4ft), **S**: 60cm (24in)
❄❄ ☼ ☼ ♈

Filipendula rubra
The emerging leaves of queen of the prairies are jagged and purple, then turn green as the tall stems rise. Its summer flowers are a light rose-pink and abundant. However, this clump-forming perennial does spread, so it needs plenty of space.

H: 2m (6ft), **S**: unlimited
❄❄ ☼ ☼

Filipendula ulmaria 'Aurea'
This golden-leaved form lightens darker plantings and makes a wonderful contrast with bronze-leaved plants. The more sun it has, the more moisture is required. Its fluffy white flowerheads are an added bonus in summer.

H: 75cm (30in), **S**: 30cm (12in)
❄❄❄ ☼ ☼

Filipendula ulmaria 'Variegata'
In this form, the dark green leaves are splashed with yellow, giving it year-long interest. Creamy-white flowers appear in summer. It tends to revert, so divide regularly in spring to remove plain green sections. Keep it moist and feed well to prevent mildew.

H: 1m (3ft), **S**: 45cm (18in)
❄❄❄ ☼ ☼

Geum rivale
The wild geum produces nodding, pink flowers in early summer. There is a white form, but 'Leonard's Variety', with larger copper-pink and cream flowers, and 'Lionel Cox', with primrose-yellow flowers, are better choices.

H: 30cm (12in), **S**: 30cm (12in)
❄❄❄ ☼ ☼

Bog plants (Gu–Li)

Gunnera manicata
With its enormous leaves (up to 2m/6ft across), this herbaceous perennial looks like a giant rhubarb. It is suitable only for large bog gardens, and needs plenty of food and water to give of its best. Protect in winter if in an exposed site.

H: 4.5m (15ft), **S**: 3m (10ft)
❄❄ ☼ ☀ ♖ ♛

Gunnera tinctoria
Unlike its huge cousin, this variety suits smaller areas. Its pleated leaves make a bold impact, but it needs other large plants to keep it company. To protect the plant over winter, fold the leaves over the crown in late autumn.

H: 2m (6ft), **S**: 1.5m (5ft)
❄❄ ☼ ☀

Iris chrysographes
This enchanting, damp-loving iris originates from China and has violet flowers with gold pencilling on the falls in summer. 'Rubella' has claret-coloured flowers. A form with near-black flowers is known by several names, including 'Black Knight'.

H: 45cm (18in), **S**: 23cm (9in)
❄❄❄ ☼ ☀ ♛

Iris ensata
This Japanese plant is one of the most sumptuous of all irises. The petals are held horizontally, making the summer flowers look enormous. There are single and double forms in white, pink, lavender, blue, purple, magenta, and mauve. Grow in damp loam.

H: 1m (3ft), **S**: 60cm (24in)
❄❄ ☼

Iris sibirica 'Butter and Sugar'
Iris sibirica has been known since the 16th century, but it was not until the 20th century that it received any attention from plant breeders. This variety's summer blooms have white central and yellow outer petals, held above the grassy foliage.

H: 25cm (10in), **S**: 25cm (10in)
❄❄ ☼ ♛

Iris sibirica 'Harpswell Happiness'
This lovely, delicate-looking iris has white flowers with yellow-green veining in late spring to early summer. Although it is called *I. sibirica*, this iris does not come from Siberia but from central and eastern Europe, Turkey, and Russia.

H: 75cm (30in), **S**: 30cm (12in)
❄❄ ☼ ♛

Iris sibirica *'Perry's Blue'*

This variety grows in a dense clump and produces in early summer plentiful stems of medium-blue flowers with ochre veins, which are useful for cutting. This old and tried variety makes a beautiful edging plant for small ponds.

H: 1m (3ft), **S**: 60cm (24in)
❄❄ ☼

Iris sibirica *'Shirley Pope'*

This is a grand improvement on older red-purple forms. In summer, its velvety, dark red-purple flowers are strikingly offset by white markings – the colour provides good contrast when grown with other varieties. It is a reliable performer with grassy foliage.

H: 1m (3ft), **S**: 45cm (18in)
❄❄ ☼ ♔

Iris sibirica *'Silver Edge'*

An eye-catching plant with large, exotic-looking, rich blue petals edged with white in early summer. All *sibirica* irises should be propagated by division in early spring or after flowering. Avoid splitting the plant too finely; take large divisions.

H: 1m (3ft), **S**: 60cm (24in)
❄❄ ☼ ♔

Iris sibirica *'Sky Wings'*

With its delightful, pale blue, dark-veined flowers in mid-spring, this reliable performer is an ideal partner for darker varieties. It is a good idea to remove the seedheads to prevent unwanted seedlings that may not resemble the parent plants.

H: 75cm (30in), **S**: 30cm (12in)
❄❄ ☼

Kirengeshoma palmata

Introduced from Japan in 1891, this clump-forming perennial has attractive jagged green leaves that alternate up the stem and support plentiful yellow shuttlecock-shaped blooms in early autumn. It likes chalk-free, deep soil and tolerates shade.

H: 1.2m (4ft), **S**: 75cm (30in)
❄❄ ☼ ♔

Ligularia dentata *'Desdemona'*

A robust perennial with attractive foliage and flowers. The early leaves are purple, a colour that persists on the undersides all season. Ragged bunches of dark yellow, daisy-like flowers appear in midsummer. Propagate by division in spring.

H: 1.2m (4ft), **S**: 1m (3ft)
❄❄❄ ☼ ◐ ♔

Bog plants (Li–Mi)

Ligularia przewalskii

This elegant Chinese perennial has deeply divided triangular leaves on almost black stems. In summer, these are topped by spires of small, pale yellow flowers. It is a very good background plant for drier bog gardens or the banks of streams.

H: 1.5m (5ft), **S**: 75cm (30in)
❀❀❀ ☼ ◐ ☾

Ligularia stenocephala 'The Rocket'

The heart-shaped leaves of this variety have toothed edges. Black stems carry long spikes of mid-yellow, daisy-like flowers in summer. The plant thrives in a good loam in moist conditions. Propagate by division in early spring.

H: 2m (6ft), **S**: 1.1m (3½ft)
❀❀❀ ☼ ◐ ☾

Lobelia x speciosa

This group of wet-loving summer-flowering perennials extends to more than 30 brilliantly coloured varieties, predominantly in shades of red but also in purple, pink, and white. Keep young plants frost-free in winter.

H: 75cm (30in), **S**: 20cm (8in)
❀ ☼

Lysimachia clethroides

This native of China and Japan is a distinctive-looking herbaceous perennial. Arching spikes of tiny white flowers, which look like small shepherds' crooks, appear in late summer on top of upright stems. Propagate by division.

H: 1m (3ft), **S**: unlimited
❀❀❀ ☼ ◐ ☾

Lysimachia ephemerum

This plant arrived in our gardens from southern Europe as long ago as 1730. It has rather grey, leathery foliage and erect stems that carry dense spikes of saucer-shaped, uniquely coloured grey-white summer flowers, gently veined in mauve.

H: 1m (3ft), **S**: 30cm (12in)
❀❀ ☼ ◐

Lysimachia nummularia 'Aurea'

Creeping Jenny has prostrate stems that creep over damp soil, rooting as they go. It is covered in small, golden leaves, which are so brightly coloured that they cannot be distinguished from the yellow flowers. Evergreen, it is useful at pond edges.

H: 2.5cm (1in), **S**: unlimited
❀❀ ☼ ◐ ☾

Lysimachia punctata

Dotted loosestrife is best for wild gardens, where its dense heads of bright yellow summer flowers provide a colourful show amid insignificant foliage. The form 'Alexander' has attractive, white variegated leaves.

H: 75cm (30in), **S**: 60cm (24in)

Lythrum salicaria 'Feuerkerze'

Purple loosestrife is a robust perennial with brilliant magenta-purple flowers in summer and woody stems that are resistant to wind damage. It is a good idea to deadhead the plant after flowering to prevent it from seeding everywhere.

H: 1.5m (5ft), **S**: 45cm (18in)

Matteuccia struthiopteris

The shuttlecock fern is one of the loveliest of its kind. Mature crowns have symmetrically arranged fronds that emerge in spring. It does not tolerate drying winds. It increases by spreading roots and will eventually fill a substantial area.

H: 1.2m (4ft), **S**: unlimited

Miscanthus sinensis 'Gracillimus'

A deciduous perennial grass made up of masses of slender green leaves with a central silver stripe that form tight clumps. Fluffy flowerheads appear in late summer. It looks particularly attractive planted around the edges of medium-sized ponds.

H: 1.3m (4½ft), **S**: 60cm (24in)

Miscanthus sinensis 'Silberfeder'

Miscanthus are not invasive and make attractive grasses beside ponds and in bog gardens. This form has long green leaves with silver stripes down the centre and, in autumn, produces white plumes held above the foliage.

H: 2.5m (8ft), **S**: 1.2m (4ft)

Miscanthus sinensis 'Variegatus'

The broad white-striped leaves of this miscanthus arch gracefully from strong stems and contrast well with plain-leaved plants. Sprays of creamy-white flowers appear in autumn, providing late-season interest.

H: 1.5m (5ft), **S**: 1m (3ft)

Bog plants (Mi–Pr)

Miscanthus sinensis 'Zebrinus'

This miscanthus has broader leaves than others, and makes a lush clump. As the season develops, transverse golden bands appear on the leaves. Tall stems produce feathery sprays of silky flowers in autumn, which persist through winter.

H: 2m (6ft), **S**: 1.1m (3½ft)
❋❋❋ ☼ ◑ ♛

Onoclea sensibilis

The sensitive fern is so-called because it dies back fast at the first frost. Its leathery fronds are mid-green but there is an attractive form with bronze edging to the new fronds. Propagate by division in early spring.

H: 60cm (24in), **S**: unlimited
❋❋ ◑ ♛

Osmunda regalis

The royal fern is an increasingly rare and very imposing British native. It looks best planted by streams and pools where there is plenty of moisture and space. The roots are the source of osmunda fibre, once used as a growing medium for orchids.

H: 1.5m (5ft), **S**: 1.2m (4ft)
❋❋❋ ☼ ◑ ♛

Persicaria 'James Compton'

This is an attractive foliage plant with crimson-coloured leaves emerging in late spring. As the season progresses, the leaves turn olive-green, which sets off a central brown chevron. It makes a good companion for ferns. Propagate by cuttings in summer.

H: 1.1m (3½ft), **S**: 45cm (18in)
❋❋ ☼ ◑

Persicaria polymorpha

An imposing, non-invasive plant that grows happily in herbaceous borders as well as beside ponds. It has large long pointed leaves on stout hollow stems that carry a froth of white flowers from midsummer to early autumn.

H: 2.5m (8ft), **S**: 1.2m (4ft)
❋❋ ☼ ◑

Persicaria virginiana 'Painter's Palette'

This variety gets its name from the colourful foliage – small, pale yellow leaves are splashed with green and have a central, reddish-brown chevron. Its bright, almost garish, colours brighten up the garden in summer.

H: 60cm (24in), **S**: 45cm (18in)
❋❋ ◑

Petasites japonicus *var.* giganteus

This highly invasive plant is only suitable for planting beside very large pools. Greenish flowers appear on naked stems in early spring, followed by huge umbrella-like leaves on robust, grey stems. Propagate by division in spring.

H: 1.2m (4ft), **S**: unlimited
❄❄❄ ☼ ☀

Physostegia virginiana

False dragon's head or obedient plant is a deciduous, spreading perennial with showy spikes of rose-pink or purple flowers in late summer. Increase by division in early spring. The variety 'Vivid' is worth seeking out for its superb flower colour.

H: 1.2m (4ft), **S**: 60cm (24in)
❄❄ ☼ ☀

Podophyllum hexandrum

This perennial's beautiful lobed toothed leaves are splashed bronze and brown. They emerge in late spring looking like furled umbrellas. White flowers in late spring to summer are followed by large fruit, the colour and size of tomatoes.

H: 45cm (18in), **S**: 25cm (10in)
❄❄ ☀

Primula alpicola

This deciduous bog primula produces nodding fragrant yellow bells with almost-white centres, carried in a loose mop in early summer. There are pure white-flowered forms and also a violet one. Propagate from seed or by division after flowering.

H: 45cm (18in), **S**: 15cm (6in)
❄❄ ☼ ☀ ♆

Primula beesiana

This candelabra primula is a dramatic sight in summer when it bears magenta-lilac flowers on stout whitish-green stems. It is a deciduous or semi-evergreen perennial with mid-green, toothed leaves that have red midribs.

H: 60cm (24in), **S**: 30cm (12in)
❄❄ ☼ ☀

Primula florindae

The deciduous Himalayan cowslip has robust stems that carry heads of fragrant bell-shaped yellow flowers in midsummer. There are several colour variants, some with bright scarlet flowers, others with orange and ginger blooms.

H: 1m (3ft), **S**: 60cm (24in)
❄❄ ☼ ☀ ♆

Bog plants (Pr–Ro)

Primula 'Inverewe'

This magnificent semi-evergreen candelabra primula is sterile, so it can be propagated only by division in spring. Its tall, stately stems carry whorls of bright vermilion flowers that look like miniature light bulbs. Rosettes of leaves are green all winter.

H: 1m (3ft), **S**: 30cm (12in)
❄❄ ☼ ◐ ⟡ ♈

Primula japonica 'Miller's Crimson'

A deciduous candelabra primula with brownish-crimson flowers that are carried in whorls up the stem. Grow in a rich loam and propagate from seed, bearing in mind that only about three-quarters of seedlings will come true.

H: 60cm (24in), **S**: 25cm (10in)
❄❄ ☼ ◐ ⟡ ♈

Primula japonica 'Postford White'

A deciduous primula bearing white flowers with an attractive pink eye. Plant in a drift for a dramatic effect in late spring. Collect ripe seed in summer for planting in seed trays in spring. About three-quarters of plants will come true from seed.

H: 60cm (24in), **S**: 25cm (10in)
❄❄ ☼ ◐ ⟡ ♈

Primula prolifera

An evergreen candelabra primula from China that produces whorls of rich yellow flowers on stout stems in early summer. It will colonize profusely in damp situations. Propagate from seed or by division after flowering.

H: 1m (3ft), **S**: 30cm (12in)
❄❄ ☼ ◐ ⟡ ♈

Primula pulverulenta

This deciduous candelabra primula is characterized by white-coated stems that appear silver. The flowers open in late spring, and are a rich crimson-purple with orange eyes. There is a sterile form, 'Bartley Pink', which has shell-pink flowers.

H: 60cm (24in), **S**: 25cm (10in)
❄❄ ◐ ⟡ ♈

Primula rosea

A deciduous primula from the Himalayas that carries in early spring loose heads of rose-pink flowers above pale green foliage. Its small size makes it ideal for damp places in the rockery or beside small water features. Increase by division.

H: 23cm (9in), **S**: 20cm (8in)
❄❄ ◐ ⟡ ♈

Primula secundiflora

A sturdy evergreen or semi-evergreen primula that looks like a large, wine-purple cowslip. It has silvery stems with slightly lop-sided flowerheads in early summer. Leave plants to clump up for two to three years, then divide after flowering.

H: 75cm (30in), **S**: 25cm (10in)
❄❄ ☼ ☀

Primula sikkimensis

From Nepal, Sikkim, and western China, this primula has clusters of simple yellow bells in late spring and early summer that are held well above the green foliage. It is sweetly scented and well worth growing, but not very long-lived.

H: 60cm (24in), **S**: 30cm (12in)
❄❄ ☼ ☀ ♈

Rheum 'Ace of Hearts'

A decorative, but inedible, rhubarb, ideal for situations where a broad-leaved effect is wanted, such as among smaller ferns. Heart-shaped leaves are supported on thick dark purple-red stems, a colour that also appears on the main leaf veins.

H: 1.2m (4ft), **S**: 90cm (36in)
❄❄ ☼ ☀

Rheum palmatum

The leaves of this large inedible rhubarb reach up to 1m (3ft) across, and are a wonderful, dark purple-bronze colour when they emerge in spring, turning green as they mature. Off-white flowers are carried on tall stems. Propagate from seed in spring.

H: 1.2m (4ft), **S**: 2.5m (8ft)
❄❄ ☼ ☀

Rheum palmatum 'Atropurpureum'

This form has bronze-coloured young leaves, keeping a red coloration on the undersides as the foliage turns green with age. Bright magenta flowers are produced in early summer. Propagate by division in spring.

H: 1.2m (4ft), **S**: 2.5m (8ft)
❄❄ ☼ ☀ ♈

Rodgersia pinnata

A superb foliage plant from China whose large crinkled green leaves are held in pairs up the stem. The tall white or pinkish-white flowerheads, reminiscent of astilbes, are produced in early summer. Plant in a good loam.

H: 1m (3ft), **S**: 1.2m (4ft)
❄❄❄ ☼ ☀

Bog plants (Ro–Tr)

Rodgersia podophylla
In this species, the leaves all emerge at the top of the stem to create, somewhat fancifully, a large foot-like effect. They are a deep lustrous bronze when they first unfurl in late spring. Creamy-white flower spikes appear in early summer.

H: 1m (3ft), **S**: 1.2m (4ft)
❋❋❋ ☀ ◐ ♈ ♛

Rodgersia 'Parasol'
A recent introduction, the leaves are similar to *R. podophylla* but are narrower and greener, so that the plant resembles an umbrella. The flowers are greenish-white. It is useful for providing background interest in a damp garden.

H: 1.2m (4ft), **S**: 1.5m (5ft)
❋❋❋ ☀ ◐

Rodgersia podophylla 'Rotlaub'
This form is smaller than the species; the foliage is a similar shape but a much deeper shade of red when it emerges in spring. The colour persists for some time, making this plant an excellent companion for other forms. Propagate by division in spring.

H: 75m (2½ft), **S**: 1.2m (4ft)
❋❋❋ ☀ ◐

Rodgersia sambucifolia
This plant resembles *R. pinnata* (*see p.151*) but is much larger. Its leaves are like giant versions of those of a horse chestnut tree. A mature clump is a fine sight, especially when the creamy-white flower spikes come into their own in early summer.

H: 1.2m (4ft), **S**: 2m (6ft)
❋❋❋ ☀ ◐

Salvia uliginosa
The bog sage is a clump-forming perennial with brilliant sky-blue flowers that appear in late summer and autumn. Attractive green nettle-shaped leaves are produced on tall stems. Its roots need protection in winter.

H: 2m (6ft), **S**: unlimited
❋ ☀ ♛

Sanguisorba canadensis
From wet meadows and swamps in eastern North America, this plant has lush green foliage on strong, branching stems. Bottle-brush-shaped white flower spikes appear in early autumn, just as other flowers are fading.

H: 1.5m (5ft), **S**: 60cm (24in)
❋❋ ☀

Selinum wallichianum
E.A. Bowles described this as the most beautiful of ferny-leaved plants. It looks like a cow parsley, with large flat white flowerheads from midsummer to early autumn. Each little flower has black anthers. Grow it in a good loam.

H: 1.2m (4ft), **S**: 75cm (30in)
❄❄ ☼

Senecio smithii
This is an interesting deciduous perennial with long greyish-green leaves topped by spires of yellow-eyed, white daisies. It forms good clumps and is best propagated by division in spring. Plant it in rich, moist soil alongside ligularias.

H: 1.2m (4ft), **S**: 75cm (30in)
❄❄ ☼ ◐

Trollius chinensis
This Far Eastern species has deep gold, almost orange, flowers in midsummer. Each has a shallow bowl of petals filled with a mass of stamens. The flowers are held on tall stems and appear to glow in the evening light.

H: 1m (3ft), **S**: 45cm (18in)
❄❄❄ ☼ ◐

Trollius x cultorum 'Alabaster'
The beautiful globe flower is a delicate ivory, so unusual that it always excites comment. It is a good plant for smaller pools and bog gardens and is an excellent companion for *Primula prolifera*, some irises, and ferns.

H: 45cm (18in), **S**: 25cm (10in)
❄❄ ☼ ◐

Trollius x cultorum 'Orange Princess'
The shape of the flower as well as its colour reflect this hybrid's *T. chinensis* parentage. Deep orange flowers are borne on tall stems well above the basal foliage. It looks good in front of plants with bronze leaves.

H: 1m (3ft), **S**: 45cm (18in)
❄❄❄ ☼ ◐

Trollius europaeus
This clump-forming perennial has been in our gardens since 1581. Its flowers appear in late spring and have incurved pale yellow petals. Propagate by division in autumn or early spring. It grows anywhere where the soil does not dry out.

H: 60cm (24in), **S**: 30cm (12in)
❄❄❄ ☼ ◐

Suppliers

Bennetts Water Gardens
(National Collection of Water Lilies)
Putton Lane
Chickerel
Weymouth
Dorset DT3 4AF
Tel: 01305 785150
Email: info@waterlily.co.uk
www.waterlily.co.uk

Binny Plants
(Iris, grasses and ferns)
Binny Estate
Ecclesmachen
West Lothian EH52 6NL
Tel: 01506 858931
Email: info@binnyplants.co.uk
www.binnyplants.co.uk

Bowden Hostas
(National Collection of Modern
Hybrid Hostas)
Sticklepath
Okehampton
Devon EX20 2NL
Tel: 01837 840989
Email: info@bowdenhostas.com
Website: www.bowdenhostas.com

Cleve West Landscape Design
(Water garden design)
Navigator House
60 High Street
Hampton Wick
Surrey KT1 4DB
Tel: 020 8977 3522
Email: info@clevewest.com
www.clevewest.com

Crocus.co.uk
Nursery Court
London Road
Windlesham
Surrey GU20 6LQ
Tel: 0870 787 1414
www.crocus.co.uk

Dorset Water Lilies
Yeovil Road
Halstock
Yeovil
Somerset BA22 9RR
Tel: 01935 891668
Email: dorsetwaterlily.co.uk

Endsleigh Gardens
Milton Abbot
Tavistock
Devon PL19 OPG
Tel: 01822 870235
Email: info@endsleigh-gardens.com
www.endsleigh-gardens.com

Hall Farm Nursery
(Marginals and bog plants)
Vicarage Lane
Kinnerley
Nr Oswestry
Shropshire SY10 8DH
Tel: 01691 682135
Email: hallfarmnursery@ukonline.
  co.uk
www.hallfarmnursery.co.uk

Honeysome Aquatic Nursery
(Open by appointment only)
The Row
Sutton
Nr Ely
Cambridgeshire CB6 2PB
Tel: 01353 778889

Lilies Water Gardens
Broad Lane
Newdigate
Surrey RH5 5AT
Tel: 01306 631064
Email: mail@lilieswatergardens.co.uk
www.lilieswatergardens.co.uk

Longstock Park Nursery
(Aquatics and ferns)
Longstock
Stockbridge
Hampshire SO20 6EH
Tel: 01264 810894
Email: longstocknursery@
leckfordestate.co.uk
www.longstocknursery.co.uk

Merebrook Water Plants
Merebrook Farm
Hanley Swan
Worcestershire WR8 ODX
Tel: 01684 310950
Email: enquiries@pondplants.co.uk
www.pondplants.co.uk

Mickfield Hostas
The Poplars
Mickfield
Stowmarket
Suffolk IP14 5LH
Tel: 01449 711576
Email: mickfieldhostas@btconnect.
  com
www.mickfieldhostas.co.uk

Mickfield Watergarden Centre Ltd
(Hardy aquatics and bog plants)
Debenham Road
Mickfield
Stowmarket
Suffolk IP14 5LP
Tel: 01449 711336
Email: mike@mickfield.co.uk
www.watergardenshop.co.uk

Ninesprings Nursery
(Aquatic plants and design advice)
The Weir
Whitchurch
Hampshire RG28 7RA
Tel: 01256 892837
Email: graham@gyrdan.demon.co.uk

Outside Inside Aquatics
5A Knox Place
Haddington
East Lothian EH41 4DY
Tel: 01620 829299
Email: outsideinsidefish@ btinternet.
   com

Paul Bromfield Aquatics
(Water lilies and aquatics)
Maydencroft Lane
Gosmore
Hitchin
Hertfordshire SG4 7QD
Tel: 01462 457399
Email: info@bromfieldaquatics.co.uk
www.bromfieldaquatics.co.uk

Penlan Perennials
(Aquatics, bog plants and ferns)
Penlan Farm
Penrhiwpal
Llandysul
Ceredigion SA44 5QH
Tel: 01239 851244
Email: rcain@penlanperennials.co.uk
www.penlanperennials.co.uk

PW Plants
(Bamboos and grasses)
'Sunnyside'
Heath Road
Kenninghall
Norfolk NR16 2DS
Tel: 01953 888212
Email: pw@hardybamboo.com
www.hardybamboos.com

Rowden Gardens
(National Collections of Caltha and
Water Iris)
Brentor
Tavistock
Devon
PL19 0NG
Tel: 01822 810275
Email: rowdengardens@btopenworld.
   co.uk
www.rowdengardens.com

Stapeley Water Gardens Ltd
(National Collection of Water Lilies)
London Road
Stapeley
Nantwich
Cheshire CW5 7LH
Tel: 01270 623868
Email: info@stapeleywg.com
www.stapeleywg.com

**Wasserpflanzenkulturen Eberhard
Schuster**
(Mail Order water lilies and aquatic
plants)
Kladower Weg 6
Augustenhof
19089 Crivitz
Germany
Tel: 00 49 3863 222705
Email: eberhard.Schuster@t-online.de
www.wasserpflanzen-schuster.de

The Water Garden
(Water lilies and aquatics)
Hinton Parva
Swindon
Wiltshire SN4 ODH
Tel: 01793 790558
Email: watergardens@supanet.com
www.thewatergarden.co.uk

**Water Meadow Nursery and
Herb Farm**
(Water lilies and aquatic plants)
Cheriton
Nr Alresford
Hampshire SO24 0QB
Tel: 01962 771895
Email: plantaholic@onetel.com
www.plantaholic.co.uk

Water Wych Ltd
(Chemical-free water clearing device
– correspondence only)
Wychwood
Farnham Road
Odiham
Hook
Hampshire RG29 1HS
Tel: 01962 774055
Email: info@waterwych.co.uk
www.waterwych.co.uk

World of Water
(Nationwide water gardening centres)
Tel: 01580 243 333
www.worldofwater.com

Index

Index

Acknowledgements

The publisher would like to thank the following for their kind permission to reproduce their photographs:

(Key: a-above; b-below/bottom; c-centre; l-left; r-right; t-top)

8: DK Images: Steve Wooster/RHS Chelsea Flower Show 2005 (b). **9:** John Glover. **10:** DK Images: Mark Winwood/Hampton Court Flower Show 2005/ The Elementals Garden/Designer: Anny Konig (t), Steve Wooster/RHS Chelsea Flower Show 2005/ The Chelsea Pensioners Garden/Designer: Julian Dowle (b). **11:** John Glover: RHS Wisley, Surrey (t). Derek St Romaine: RHS Tatton Park/Designers: Katie Dines & Steve Day (br). **12:** Leigh Clapp: Designer: Ann-Marie Barkai. **13:** Leigh Clapp: (c). DK Images: Steve Wooster/RHS Chelsea Flower Show 2005/Designer: Claire Whitehouse (b). **14:** Derek St Romaine: (t); Harpur Garden Library:Jerry Harpur: Julian Elliot, Cape Town, RSA (c). Modeste Herwig: Family de Ruigh/Designer: Modeste Herwig (b). **15:** The Garden Collection: Liz Eddison/Tatton Park Flower Show 2005/Designer: Jill Brindle. **16:** DK Images: Mark Winwood/Hampton Court Flower Show 2005 (t). The Garden Collection: Liz Eddison/RHS Chelsea Flower Show 2005/Designer: Andy Sturgeon (b). **17:** Andrew Lawson: Hampton Court Flower Show 2000. Designer: Philippa O'Brien (tl), Helen Fickling (tr), Clive Nichols: Designer: Mark Laurence (b). **18:** The Garden Collection: Gary Rogers/RHS Chelsea Flower Show 2005/Designer: Christopher Bradley-Hole (t), Marie O'Hara/RHS Chelsea Flower Show 2005/Designer: Sir Terence Conran (b). **19:** The Garden Collection: Liz Eddison/Tatton Park Flower Show 2002/ Designers: Chapman, Byrne-Daniel (t); Liz Eddison/Tatton Park Flower Show 2005/ Designer: Jill Brindle (bl); Liz Eddison/RHS Chelsea Flower Show 2005/Designer: David Macqueen-Orangenbleu (br). Andrew Lawson: Sculpture: Bridget McCrum (c). **20:** DK Images: Steve Wooster/Hampton Court Flower Show 2002/Japanese Garden Society/ Maureen Busby Garden Designs. **21:** John Glover: (t), Leigh Clapp: Mittens Garden (c). DK Images: Mark Winwood/Capel Manor/

Designer: Steve Wooster (b). **22:** John Glover: RHS Chelsea Flower Show. Designer Roger Platt (t), The Garden Collection: Liz Eddison (bl); Michelle Garrett (br). **23:** Clive Nichols/Chelsea Flower Show 1998. **24:** John Glover: Hampton Court Flower Show/Designer: Guy Farthing (t), The Garden Collection: Michelle Garrett (b). **25:** S & O Mathews Photography: (tl), The Garden Collection: Liz Eddison/RHS Chelsea Flower Show 1999/Designer: Chris Gregory (tr), DK Images: Mark Winwood. Capel Manor/ Designer: Steve Wooster (bl); Mark Winwood/Capel Manor/Gardening Which? (br). **28:** DK Images: Steve Wooster/RHS Chelsea Flower Show 2005/ Designer: Julian Dowle (l); Steve Wooster/ RHS Chelsea Flower Show 2001/The Blue Circle Garden, Designer: Carole Vincent (r). **29:** DK Images: Steve Wooster/RHS Chelsea Flower Show 2005/Designer: Marney Hall (l). **30:** Clive Nichols: Designer: Lucy Smith (l). **31:** John Glover: Designed by Alan Titchmarsh (r). **36:** Clive Nichols: Designer: Ulf Nordfjell (l), DK Images: Steve Wooster/RHS Chelsea Flower Show 2005/Designer: Carol Smith (r). **37:** DK Images: Mark Winwood. Hampton Court Flower Show 2005. Le Jardin Perdu. Dorset Water Lily Company (r); Mark Winwood/Hampton Court Flower Show 2005/'Time to Reflect'/Lilies Water Gardens (l). **39:** John Glover: Hampton Court Flower Show 2003/ Designers: May and Watts (tr). Clive Nichols: Designer: Mark Laurence (tl); Garen & Security Lighting (br). Derek St Romaine: Designer: Phil Nash for Robert van den Hurk (bl). **40:** Harpur Garden Library/ Jerry Harpur: Designer: Ursel Gut, Germany (l). **41:** Derek St Romaine: Mr & Mrs Kelsall, Gt. Barr, Birmingham (r). **42:** Steve Wooster/RHS Chelsea Flower Show 2001 (t), Clive Nichols: Designer: Fiona Barratt (c), DK Images: Mark Winwood/Capel Manor College/Designer: Elizabeth Ramsden (b);. **43:** Derek St Romaine: RHS Chelsea Flower Show 1997 /Designer: Andrea Parsons (t), DK Images: Steve Wooster/RHS Chelsea Flower Show 2005/Designer: John Carmichael (c); Steve Wooster/RHS Chelsea Flower Show 2002 (b). **70–71:** DK Images: Steve Wooster/ RHS Chelsea Flower Show 2001/The Blue

Circle Garden, Designer: Carole Vincent. **72:** John Glover. **78:** Andrew Lawson: RHS Chelsea Flower Show 2003. Designer: Marney Hall. **82:** Andrew Lawson: RHS Chelsea Flower Show 1999/Designer: Carol Klein. **83–85:** Mark Winwood. **95:** Derek St Romaine. **97:** Andrew Lawson: Torie Chugg/ RHS Tatton Park 2005/Designer Katie Dines. **98:** Garden World Images: (bl). **99:** DK Images: Steve Wooster/ RHS Chelsea Flower Show 2005/ Designer: Claire Whitehouse. **101:** The Garden Collection: Liz Eddison/Designers: Katie Hines & Steve Day. **103:** Garden Picture Library: Ron Sutherland/Owner: Mike Paul. **104:** Garden Picture Library: Friedrich Strauss (bl). **105:** Garden Picture Library: Friedrich Strauss. **109:** DK Images: Steve Wooster/Hampton Court Flower Show/The Reflective Garden/Designer: Alison Armour Wilson (bl). **111:** Jonathan Newman, Centre for Ecology and Hydrology. **113:** RHS Wisley/ Tim Sandall, Holt Studios International: Phil McLean/ FLPA (tr). **118:** Clive Nichols: Designer: Richard Coward (t). **122:** Andrew Lawson: (t). **126:** crocus.co.uk (bl), **132:** Garden World Images: (tl). **140:** Garden Picture Library: John GLover (tr). **142:** Garden World Images: (br). **145:** Garden World Images: (bc). **148:** crocus.co.uk (bc). **151:** Garden World Images: (bc); Gary Dunlop, Newtonards, Co. Down, N. Ireland (br). **152:** Gary Dunlop Newtonards, Co. Down, N. Ireland (tc).

All other images © Dorling Kindersley For further information see: www.dkimages.com

Dorling Kindersley would also like to thank the following:
Editors for Airedale Publishing: Helen Ridge, Fiona Wild, Mandy Lebentz *Designers for Airedale Publishing*: Elly King, Murdo Culver *Index*: Michèle Clarke

Gardening Which? (www.which.co.uk) and Capel Manor College (www.capel. ac.uk) for photography locations.

World of Water (www.worldofwater.com) for supplying materials for the bubble feature on pp.56–9.